THIS
BOOK
WAS
MADE
POSSIBLE
BY:

SACRAMENTO BUNGALOW
HERITAGE ASSOCIATION

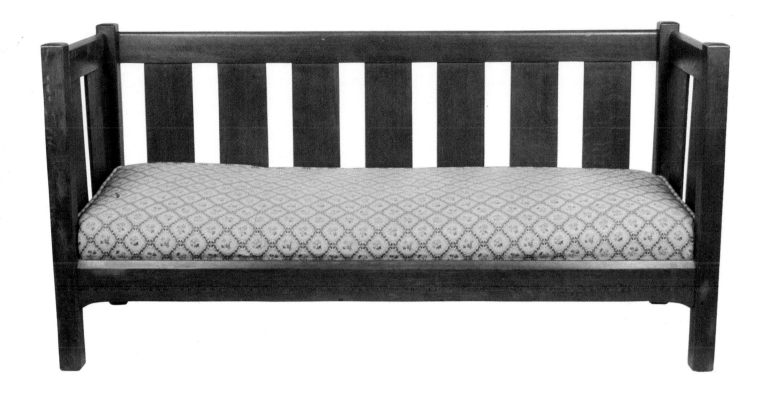

Mission Furniture

Furniture of the American Arts and Crafts Movement

Paul A. Royka

4880 Lower Valley Road, Atglen, PA 19310

Dedication

To my wonderful wife, Deborah, who has persevered, sacrificed, and supported my work on these books, my mother, Margaret, who has always helped me achieve my dreams, and in memory of my father, Robert, who taught me to take my own path.

Book Design by: Blair Loughrey

ISBN: 0-88740-987-3
Printed in Hong Kong
1 2 3 4

Published by Schiffer Publishing Ltd.
4880 Lower Valley Road
Atglen, PA 19310
Phone: (610) 593-1777; Fax: (610) 593-2002
E-mail: Schifferbk@aol.com
Please write for a free catalog.
This book may be purchased from the publisher.
Please include $3.95 for shipping.

Please try your bookstore first.

We are interested in hearing from authors
with book ideas on related subjects.

Preface

This book is titled with the now taboo label "mission furniture" because it is still the most common expression for this style of furniture today. The reason for the taboo is that mission furniture is more than a style. It is an important piece of the design reform known as the American Arts and Crafts movement. This furniture is not a copying of a former style, but a new expression designed to express a philosophy of life, embodying it in honest and simple environments.

The Arts and Crafts Movement in America coincided with the hey-day of the Industrial Revolution. As machines took over the workplace and the skills of immigrant workers were relegated to pressing buttons and monotonous routines, a feeling of despair entered the workforce. Today, the revival of interest in the Arts and Crafts Movement coincides with the Information Revolution in which the workforce is being replaced by computers and impersonal relations over electric wires creating "communities" in cyberspace.

The warmth of wood versus the coldness of plastic seems to be striking a chord in the hearts of the new collectors. In a day where people find dissatis-faction in their work, products are made to be replaced in a few years, and furniture stores have become amusement parks luring people into their stores with motion movies in order to sell furniture with compartments for snacks, mission furniture sparks a remembrance of a time when people worked with their hands. They were proud of the work of their hands and this can be seen in the construction details of mission furniture.

In general the interest in the field of Arts and Crafts has been strong. Prices soared to dizzying heights in 1987 and 1988 and fell quickly afterwards. Today the market is strong not just in prices but in the quality of research available to the new collector.

The prices assigned in this book are to a large extent retail prices. The items are assumed to be in pristine condition retaining their original finishes. Prices can quickly drop in half if there condition is not pristine or the finish has been altered.

Comments or inquiries can be sent to:

Design20c@aol.com or you can visit the authors web site at www.Design20c.com or write to Paul Royka, 210 Park Avenue, #295, Worcester, MA 01609

Acknowledgments

I would like to thank Skinner Inc. and the private collectors who allowed me to photograph their items. A special thanks to my editor Douglas Congdon-Martin and Stanley P. Bystrowski for his photography work including the cover.

Contents

Introduction

Defining "Arts and Crafts"

The concept of Arts and Crafts began as early as 1834 with the philosophical writings of several English artists and critics. These ideas were translated into the decorative arts of some of the leading designers of the 1870s. The phrase "Arts and Crafts" was first coined in 1888 by a student at the Royal Academy in London as an alternative to the phrase "fine arts" which spoke only of paintings and sculpture, relegating decorative arts to a second class. As the Arts and Crafts Movement developed, it became more associated with a loosely connected set of ideas rather than any specific style or social policy. The attitude of an object's creator had more to do with describing an item as "Arts and Crafts" than the object itself.

Philosophical Beginnings

It was England's artistic intelligentsia that had the greatest influence upon artisans in the United States. An avant-garde artistic challenge in the mid-nineteenth century known as the Pre-Raphaelite Movement was the germ that would radically change decorative arts. In 1848, a group of artists, including William Holman Hunt, John Everett Millias, and Dante Gabriel Rossetti, joined to create an English school of painting genuinely based on nature. At the time, the Royal Academy's School taught a rigorous technical instruction intended to create a pattern of formal ideas based upon a system of reference to classical literature and mythology. The Pre-Raphaelite artists became known as the Brotherhood, a group who emphasized that the post-Renaissance style was detrimental to the world of art.

The two strongest voices for this view, besides the artists themselves, were August Welby Northmore Pugin (1812-1852) and John Ruskin (1819-1900). In 1834, Pugin published *Contrasts* a work in which he discusses the connection between architecture and life. He wrote about of the purity of medieval cathedrals and rural life, contrasting it with the visual and spiritual ugliness of the industrial age. His works contributed to the revival of the Gothic school of architecture and the behaviorist view of architecture prevalent in American architects such as Frank Lloyd Wright.

John Ruskin, Slade Professor of Art at Oxford University, was the most influential of all Victorian writers on the arts. He vigorously attacked the Royal Academy School's view in support of post-Renaissance style. For him the concept of a "School of Design" was impossible. He felt that drawing may be taught by teachers but design could only be taught by Nature itself. *The Stones of Venice* was published in 1853 and had a profound influence on both sides of the Atlantic. His views would influence every artisan in the United States:

> "Men were not intended to work with the accuracy of tools, to be precise and perfect in all their actions. If you will have that precision out of them you must unhumanise them.
>
> If you will make a man of the working creature you cannot make a tool. Let him but begin to imagine, to think, to try to do anything worth doing, and...out come all his roughness, all his incapacity...failure after failure...but out comes the whole majesty of him also."
>
> "We want one man to be always thinking, and another to be always working, and we call one man a gentleman, and the other an operative; whereas the workman ought often to be thinking, and the thinker often to be working, and both should be gentlemen, in the best sense...It would be well if all of us were good handicraftsmen in some kind, and the dishonor of manual labor done away with altogether. [We see] the degradation of the operative in to machine...It is not that men are ill fed, but that they have no pleasure in the work by which they make their bread and therefore look to wealth as the only means of pleasure."

Ruskin's writings became available to the American art community in 1851 when John Wiley published Ruskin's Pre-Raphaelite pamphlet in New York. In 1857,

Pre-Raphaelitism in America was stimulated by the exhibition of contemporary British art in New York. The exhibition, containing 356 objects, traveled to Boston. The British artist Rossetti was a key figure in bringing this exhibition about. Two magazines, *The Crayon* and *The New Path* would disseminate Ruskin's ideas to the general public in America. The fundamental importance of Ruskin's writing in America was his ability to connect art with morality and religion through an exploration of nature. This struck a response from the general American public which already held an attitude of reverence for nature.

This response created the American Pre-Raphaelites (A.P.R.), a group of artists during the 1850's and 1860's who opposed the teachings of the National Academy in New York and the Pennsylvania Academy of Fine Arts which held similar views to the Royal Academy School in London. The A.P.R. believed that a study of nature should be completed outdoors. They opposed the Hudson River School of artists who would make sketches in pen and pencil in natural surroundings but compose the painting in a studio. The A.P.R. believed this style of painting was untrue to nature. A.P.R. practiced painting with a heightened meticulousness and specificity of detail that was good enough for a botanist. This was referred to as the Ruskinian lens. The artists removes himself from the work to allow nature to speak for itself.

Charles Eliot Norton became the direct link between Ruskin and the American. A friend of John Ruskin, he was appointed Professor of the History of Art at Harvard University in 1875 and continued this position for twenty-three years. It should be noted that this was the first position of its kind in the United States. It was only in 1867 that John Stuart Mill, as rector of the University of St. Andrews, suggested that culture in the arts be admitted as an essential portion of education. From this position, Norton was able to influence the artisans in the United States.

Philosophy Becomes Decorative Arts

As a student at Oxford University, William Morris (1834-1896) was strongly influenced by Ruskin's teachings. In 1857, at the age of 23, he collaborated in the painting of Pre-Raphaelite frescoes in the Oxford Union. By 1861, at the age of 27, Morris becomes the first to successfully incorporate the ideas of the Pre-Raphaelites into the decorative arts. He founded Morris, Marshall, Faulkner and Company later to become Morris and Company in 1875 which produced all aspects for interior furnishings including stained glass, wallpapers, fabrics and furniture. He even went as far as incorporating Pre-Raphaelite paintings into the doors of his furniture. These objects were in opposition to Victorian, post Renaissance designs, which incorporated an eclectic mix of Greek, Roman and Italian Renaissance styles, and were produced cheaply by the new machinery of the industrial revolution.

Morris's concerns were a mix of aesthetic and social reform. He believed he could improve the worker's condition in life if the worker cared about what he produced and therefore found satisfaction and pleasure in his work.

Another major English design reformer was Charles Locke Eastlake. He was the author of *Hints on Household Taste* in 1868. This book expressed the principles of simplicity, functionalism, and honesty of construction. His furniture designs were marked by a lightness unseen in Renaissance and Gothic revival forms. Veneers were scorned in favor of hand construction. Eastlake admired the way in which simple medieval furniture was made by hand . This, rather than the imitation of specific styles from the past eras, was what he sought, thereby freeing his followers from strict adherence to historical motifs.

Arthur Lasenby Liberty (1843-1917) was the founder of Liberty & Company. The company specialized in the production of textiles and interior furnishings in the Art Nouveau style (characterized by organic, undulating lines) which would become known as "Style Liberty." After a trip to Japan in 1889, he began incorporating Japanese themes into his furnishings. Liberty employed some of the most notable designers of the period including Christopher Dresser, C.F.A. Voysey and Archibald Knox.

Oriental Influences

Exhibitions during the 1860s and 1870s ignited a taste for the Oriental aesthetic. The London International Exhibition in 1862 placed on display objects collected by Sir Rutherford Alcock, the British Prime Minister to Japan, and later developed the appetite for Liberty & Company's product. The Centennial Exposition of 1876 in Philadelphia provided the general American public its first view of the new style and designers such as Greene and Greene viewed the World's Columbian Exposition in Chicago which featured a Japanese Pavilion.

Arts and Crafts Movement and American Architecture

In general, there were three main schools of architecture practicing Arts and Crafts ideals in the United States. The New England school which consisted of glorious shingled homes along the coastline and the mansions of Boston's business men built in the mid section of Massachusetts. Many of these homes were the work of Willard Brown who graduated from Harvard in 1892 and Massachusetts Institute of Technology in 1894. Willard Brown opened his office in Lexington, Massachusetts in 1902 and quickly received the commissions from Boston's leading families. Brown often utilized Grueby tiles in his interiors and created elaborate Japanese courtyards utilizing Gustav Stickley furniture and lighting fixtures. His ultimate bungalow was called Journey's End. This bungalow was set upon the highest point in Lexington. It had an outdoor living room that was 85 x 14 feet which could be enclosed to be used as an extra apartment. The Japanese courtyard was enclosed in the center of the house. It contained a stone basin with fountains, at the foot of which glass prisms are set and the entire room was illuminated by electric lights under the water. Many of Brown's ultimate bungalows were destroyed over the years and his work forgotten until recent years.

The Prairie School of architecture consisted of a group of architects who constructed buildings emphasizing the horizontal plane and utilized the concept of unity between a building and its interior. Its leading proponents were Frank Lloyd Wright, George Washington Maher, and George Grant Elmslie. Wright stated in his autobiography that "very few of the houses were anything but painful to me after the clients moved in and helplessly dragged the horrors of the old order along after them." Wright began to design the furniture for his buildings and used Stickley furniture in the homes when his clients could no longer afford his designs.

The California school of architecture consisted of bungalows that utilized Oriental, Swiss, Dutch and Spanish Colonial Revival design motifs. They primarily consisted of single floor plans with central living rooms, porches and pergolas. The leading architects in California were Alfred Heineman, Ross Montgomery, Frederick Roehrig, Henry Wilson and, most notably, the Greene brothers. Charles and Henry Greene studied the same courses that Willard Brown studied at Massachusetts Institute of Technology. In 1893 Greene and Greene settled in Pasadena and began construction ultimate bungalows between 1907 and 1909. The ultimate bungalows designed during this period incorporated elaborate use of exotic woods such as teak and ebony in both the interior wall treatments and furnishings. They are considered by many to be the finest examples of the Arts and Crafts Movement in America.

The spread of architecture inspired by the Arts and Crafts Movement created a demand for mission style furniture. Gustav Stickley's *Craftsman Magazine* provided house plans and complete interior drawings which utilized his textiles, lighting devices, metalwork and furniture. New manufacturers such as Young, Limbert, and the Stickley companies were created to keep up with the demand and old companies began to introduce the style to stay competitive. By the 1920s the bungalow fever which had swept the country was over. Gustav Stickley filed bankruptcy in 1915 and most companies including L. & J.G. Stickley returned to producing a colonial revival style of furniture.

Helpful Details

The large variety of companies that produced mission furniture sometimes makes identification difficult. In general, pieces were signed with paper labels or small painted decals. Both were easily worn away by steam heat, the removal of old fabric seats or the spring cleaning with shellac instead of wax. Even companies like Limbert that utilized brand marks didn't sign every piece. There was quality control but anomalies always appear. For instance this Harden chair displays all the features that one would expect to find on a Gustav Stickley chair: a v-back, same corbel form, pegged construction between corbel and leg post. The only problem is that the chair retains its original paper label by the Harden Company.

The following photos show structural details of some of Young, Limbert, Harden, L.& J.G. Stickley and Gustav Stickley chairs. Dealers often compare structural details such as how adjusting mechanisms work, forms of corbels, forms of tenons, size of pegs, form of glue blocks and seat arrangements.

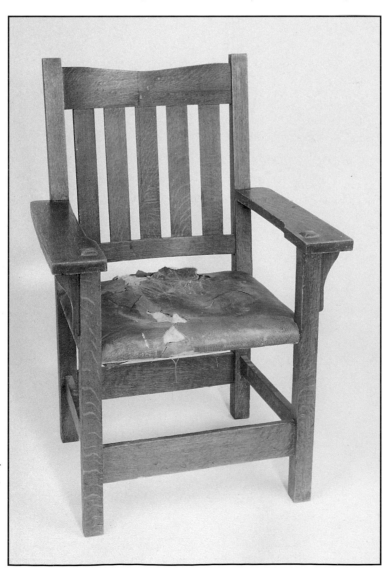

Harden chair
with v-back.

Harden corbel that is exactly the
same as a Gustav Stickley design.

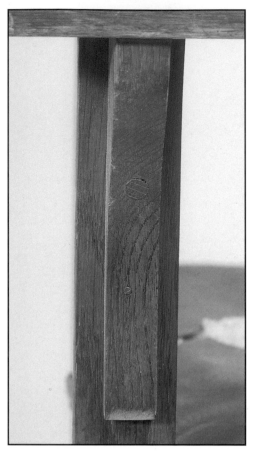

Detail of peg on Harden
corbel like Gustav Stickley's.

J.M. Young paper label.

Adjusting mechanism found
on a J.M. Young Morris chair.

Adjusting mechanism and seat arrangement for J.M. Young Morris chair.

Corbel on J.M. Young chair.

Tenon on J.M. Young chair.

Adjusting mechanism on Limbert Morris chair.

Corbel on Limbert chair.

Tenon on Limbert chair.

L. & J.G. Stickley adjusting mechanism.

L. & J.G. Stickley glue block.

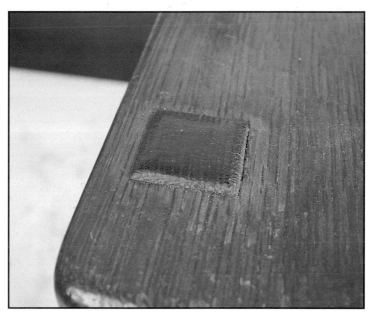

L.& J.G. Stickley corbel on a chair.

L. & J.G. Stickley tenon.

Seat frame for a Gustav Stickley Morris chair.

Tenons and pegs on a Gustav Stickley chair.

Gustav Stickley corbel.

Gustav Stickley tenon.

Gustav Stickley pyramid tack on a dining chair.

Pegs and tenons on a Harden Morris chair.

Glue block on a Harden Morris chair.

Harden arm arrangement with the small tenon.

Mission Furniture Terms

Apron: the rail along the base of sideboards or china cabinets or around the seats of chairs which can incorporate decorative elements such as arches.

Bungalow: an architectural style based upon the amalgamation of several different Indian house types which were further developed in England and America which incorporate open porches and central living rooms which emphasize simple living spaces.

Butterfly keys: a type of wooden joint that resembles the wings of a butterfly used to hold two boards together.

Chamfered boards: the joining of boards end to end with beveled edges which create a joint resembling a "v".

Corbel: a transitional element that projects from a vertical surface to a horizontal surface usually found between a chair leg and arm.

Dovetail: a flaring tenon and a mortise into which it fits tightly making an interlocking joint between two pieces of wood.

Fumed: a process in which the color of a finish is obtained by placing a piece of oak in an enclosed space with ammonia. The reaction between ammonia and the tannin in the wood creates a dark brown color which permeates the wood.

Hand-hammered: a style of metal work which resembles small dimples usually found on the handles and hinges of pieces of furniture.

H-back: the form of the back of chairs designed by Gustav Stickley that resemble an "H".

Inlay: ornamental motifs made of pewter, mother-of-pearl, and exotic woods which are placed flush with the surface of boards usually found on slats, chair legs or doors of pieces of furniture.

Key and tenon: a joint found usually on the side of bookcases, china cabinets and library tables in which a piece of wood is placed through a tenon to hold a joint in place.

Ladder back: the form of the back of a chair which resembles the steps of a ladder.

Hand-hammered pull.

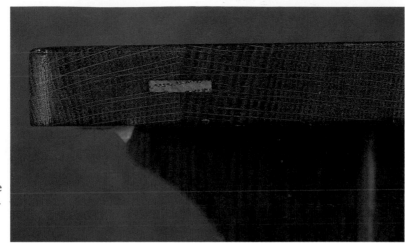

Detail of a spline
on a table top.

Mackmurdo foot: a style by the English designer Arthur Mackmurdo which was used on furniture which resembles a flared trumpet form.

Miter: a joint formed by cutting two pieces at an angle and fitting them together.

Morris chair: the name of a chair designed by the English designer William Morris that has an adjusting back which was utilized by many American furniture makers.

Mortise: a hole cut in a piece of wood to receive a projecting part (tenon).

Mullion: a slender, vertical or horizontal piece of wood which divided glass window panes on bookcases and china cabinets.

Pegs (Pins): small wooden dowels used to secure a mortise and tenon joint inside a post.

Prairie School: a regional school of architecture in the Midwestern United States which emphasized the horizontal plane and the unity of the exterior with the interior. These architects include George Elmslie, George Maher and Frank Lloyd Wright.

Shoe feet: a style which incorporates a cross section of wood that sits on the floor between the front leg and back legs of a piece of furniture.

Slats: the vertical or horizontal boards usually found on the back or sides of chairs.

Spline: a thin wood strip used between two boards to prevent warping usually found on table tops.

Stretcher: the wooden slats found on the base of chairs and tables which brace the legs.

Tenon: a projecting part cut on the end of a piece of wood for insertion into a mortise to make a joint. For example, many arms of chairs have a tenon which is created form the front leg posts passing through the arms of the chair.

U-back: a design found on the top rail of chairs which resembles a subtle "u" shape.

V-back: a design found on the top rail of chairs which resembles a "v". The design is also sometimes an inverted "v".

Key and Tenons
on the side of a
bookcase.

Furniture Companies

The Stickley Family:

Gustav, Leopold, John George, Albert and Charles.

Rare Gustav Stickley Eastwood chair, (Skinner), $20,000+.

Gustav Stickley, Craftsman Workshops, Eastwood, New York, (c.1902 - 1916).

To most people, the name Stickley conveys the idea of a simple, undecorated, and rectangular style of furniture that was made in the first quarter of the 20th century. In fact, Stickley represents the name of five different brothers, each of whom created different furniture companies. Together they would make the name famous.

The first Stickley to begin designing what was to be called Mission furniture was Gustav Stickley. Gustav was born on March 9, 1858 in Osceola, Wisconsin. His parents, Leopold and Barbara Schlaeger Stoeckel (Americanized to Stickley), came from Germany. The family lived in Wisconsin until the father, who was an alcoholic, abandoned the family. Barbara moved the family east to live with her brother, Jacob Schlaeger, in Pennsylvania. Gustav went to work to help support the family. His uncle owned a small chair factory in Brandt, Pennsylvania. Gustav recalled these early years:

"My first experience in furniture making came when I began work in a small chair factory in the hamlet of Brandt...where we made the plain wood and caned-seated chairs so much used in those days...It was the most commonplace of stereotyped work, yet from it, I can date my love for working in wood and my appreciation of the beauty and interest to be found in its natural color, texture and grain." (Smith, Mary Ann, *Gustav Stickley The Craftsman*, p. 2)

Gustav worked for his uncle until 1884. When he was 26, he and his brothers, Charles and Albert, created a business in Binghamton, New York selling retail furniture specializing in ornate black walnut furniture made in Grand Rapids. Two years later, in 1886, the Stickley Brothers Company added a chair factory to their business. Gustav recounts:

"Before any capital would be put into the concern, it was necessary to show that we were actually manufacturing, and we had no money to buy machinery. I went to a maker of broom handles who had a good turning lathe which he used only part of the time. I hired the use of this and with it blocked out the plainer parts of some very simple chairs made after the 'Shaker' model. The rest of them I made by hand, with the aid of a few simple and inexpensive machines which were placed in the loft of the store. All we had was a hand-lathe, boring machine, framing saw and chuck, and the power was transmitted by rope from a neighboring establishment. The wood in shape was dried in the sun on the tin roof of the building. The very primitiveness of this equipment, made necessary by lack of means, furnished what was really a golden opportunity to break away from the monotony of commercial forms, and I turned my attention to reproducing by hand some of the simplest and best models of the Old Colonial, Windsor and other plain chairs, and to a study of this period as a foundation for original work along the same lines...This was in 1886, and it was the beginning of the 'fancy chair' era. The reproduction of Colonial designs soon became popular, as these "fancy" chairs and rockers proved a most satisfactory substitute for the heavy and commonplace 'parlor-suits' of which people were beginning to tire." (Smith, *Ibid.*, p. 3)

Although Gustav refers to his chairs as "fancy", the pieces were much less ornate than the black walnut furniture they had been selling.

Gustav left the family firm around 1889. He entered into various business relationships which all seem to have helped create his future business. He became partners with Elgin A. Simonds and produced more colonial revival furniture. In 1891, he became vice-present of the Binghamton Street Railroad which may have been a result of his business associations. Then between 1892 and 1894, Gustav was Director of Manufacturing Operations at the New York State Prison at Auburn. Gustav used prison labor to produce furniture to be sold to the public. By 1894, the New York Legislature passed a law prohibiting the sale of products made by convicts. With this change in the law looming, Gustav worked on plans for a new furniture company in Eastwood, New York, a suburb of Syracuse. His former business partner, Simonds, joined him, and together they purchased a sight for the new firm. Between 1892 and 1896, the new Stickley-Simonds business seemed to be a success, producing furniture in English and French styles. During 1898, Gustav would become interested in the plans for an American Furniture Company that would combine all chair makers together into one huge company. The plan never materialized and it is believed that this was the year that Gustav Stickley visited Europe. The trip to Europe significantly changed Gustav Stickley's aesthetic and business practices.

Gustav Stickley would have visited sights in England which displayed the new furnishings of the Arts and Crafts Movement. It is possible that Gustav visited Morris and Company which displayed Arts and Crafts interiors. There he would have seen Morris chairs (chairs with adjustable backs), designed by William Morris, a student of John Ruskin. He may have also visited Liberty & Company which was founded by Arthur Lasenby Liberty. He specialized in Oriental decorations, Art Nouveau furnishings from France and Germany, textiles by M.H. Baillie Scott and inlaid furniture of C.F.A. Voysey, and works influenced by the Glasgow School of designers, such as Charles Rennie Mackintosh. Gustav would have been greatly influenced by Baillie Scott and Voysey's concepts of totally designed interior environments.

Stickley Brothers inlaid chair, ht. 43-3/4",
signed with Quaint brass tag, $1500.

Gustav Stickley returned from Europe with a new set of aesthetic aspirations:

"In 1900 I stopped using the standard patterns and finishes, and began to make all kinds of furniture after my own designs, independently of what other people were doing, or of any necessity to fit my designs, woods and finishes to any other factory. For about a year I experimented with more or less fantastic forms...My frequent journeys to Europe...interested me much in the decorative use of plant forms, and I followed the suggestion...After experimenting with a number of pieces, such as small tables giving in their form a conventionalized suggestion of such plants as the mallow, the sunflower and the pansy, I abandoned the idea...Conventionalized plant forms are beautiful and fitting when used solely for decoration, but anyone who starts to make a piece of furniture with a decorative form in mind, starts at the wrong end. The sole consideration at the basis of design must be the thing itself and not its ornamentation.

"The Arts and Crafts movement was more nearly in harmony with what I had in mind, but even that did not involve a return to the sturdy and primitive forms that were meant for usefulness alone, and I began to work along the lines of a direct application of the fundamental principles of structure to the designing and craftsmanship of my furniture." (Smith, *Ibid.*, p. 20)

In 1900, Gustav exhibited his new designs for furniture at the semiannual furniture trade show in Grand Rapids, Michigan. His furniture designs were given favorable reviews by *House Beautiful* and were quickly put into production by Tobey Furniture Company of Chicago. Stickley's association with Tobey was short

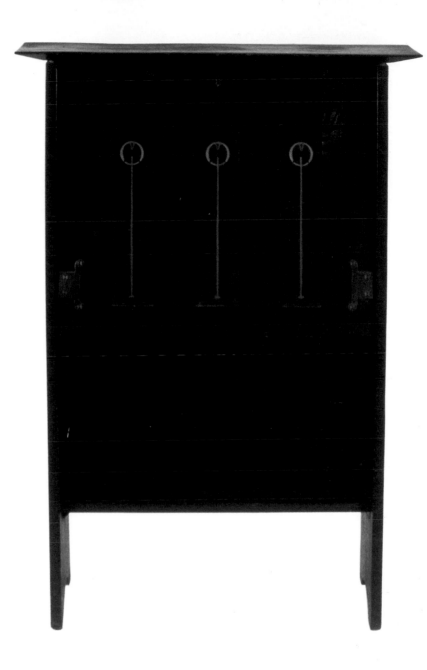

Rare Harvey Ellis designed cabinet produced by Gustav Stickley, (Skinner), $30,000+.

lived and Gustav acquired space in Syracuse to begin designing and selling his furniture independently. Gustav opened his new offices and showroom in the Crouse Stable building in Syracuse, New York. He published his first illustrated catalogue in 1900. The catalogue featured several plant stands and chairs which displayed organic forms inspired by his experiences in Europe.

Soon these organic forms would be replaced by severe rectilinear designs. At the age of 42, Gustav would begin to create his best designs. One of his earliest and most significant pieces is the Eastwood chair. The chair represents a bold change from the styles of the time. The chair used no applied ornament or carving and lacked any organic form. Instead it displayed a severe honesty in construction and proportions. The arms are massive with through tenons and clipped corners. The stretchers are massive and the back slats curve slightly to create a comfortable chair. The finish is fumed oak and the cushion is either rush or a leather cushion on a rope foundation. Gustav created a design that displayed integrity in construction and purity in form. He writes about his combination of rush and fumed oak in the first issue of *The Craftsman* magazine in 1901:

> "[The rush and oak] combination cannot be otherwise than a perfect one, as it is based upon Nature as displayed in the autumn woods."

The chair is representative of this early period of Gustav Stickley's designs from 1901 to 1904 in which the designs are more severe and rectilinear.

There was a debate during the period if Gustav Stickley was really the first to begin using these severe designs. George F. Clingman of the Tobey Furniture

Rare Gustav Stickley spindle settee, (Skinner), $20,000+.

Company claimed that he had given Gustav Stickley the ideas for his early rectilinear designs when they met during the Grand Rapids Furniture show. New York furniture maker Joseph P. McHugh claimed he was the first to use the term "Mission oak" to describe his furniture. What distinguishes Gustav Stickley from these other furniture makers is that he did more than just produce furniture. His furniture was the embodiment of a group of ideals which were expressed in his monthly magazine *The Craftsman*:

> "The objects which form our material environment exert upon us an influence that is not to be withstood. If we, our children and our successors are to be true citizens and integral parts of the Commonwealth, we must choose carefully the objects by which we surround ourselves; bringing our judgment to bear upon them as fully as we do upon our books, our studies and our companions. We must support an art created by the people for the people: simple, sincere and structural; an art wherein the designer and the craftsman shall be one and the same individual, creating for his own pleasure and unassailed by commercialism. It is in this spirit that the Master and Associates of the United Crafts produce their work and await results."

Gustav would spread the ideals of the Arts and Crafts movement through his magazine. The magazine published articles on such diverse subjects as American pottery companies and exhibitions, jewelry design, home building and gardening. Gustav adopted a medieval joiner's compass and the motto "Als ik kan" which roughly translates to "The best that I can" which was used by the Flemish painter Jan van Eyck. The joiner's compass and motto would appear in all his issues of *The Craftsman* and on his furniture.

In June of 1903, Gustav Stickley hired Harvey Ellis. Harvey Ellis was born in Rochester, New York in 1852. Ellis began his career as a draftsman and worked under Henry Hobson Richardson. Richardson graduated from Harvard in 1859 and entered the Ecole des Beaux-Arts in Paris in 1860. He practiced in New York and moved to Brookline, Massachusetts in 1874. One of his earliest projects was the design for the Church of Unity in Springfield, Massachusetts. The importance of Richardson's influence on Ellis is that Richardson believed the design of furniture, fixtures, and other interior elements were all part of the architects job. Ellis would incorporate this into his own work. Ellis designed a variety of homes for *The Craftsman* magazine. His interiors were harmonious with elaborately detailed color schemes:

"Here, the walls are a strong golden yellow, the ceiling the gray of the plaster, and the woodwork a rich olive green; the visible wall in the alcove for the sideboard is a dark, dull Indian red, and the floor a golden yellow, with a large moss-green rug in the center." (Smith, *Ibid.*)

Along with elaborate color schemes, Ellis designed furniture for Gustav Stickley. His designs were lighter and more graceful than those of his employer. He scaled the proportions down and added arches to lighten the effect of Gustav's early forms. The inlaid decorations accented the structural lines of the furniture and were usually stylized foliate designs made of pewter, copper and various woods. After working for Gustav Stickley for only seven months, Ellis died at the age of 52. Known as the "vagrant genius" who traveled from place to place working as an architect, Ellis was greatly respected. An article in the April 1908 *Architectural Review*, spoke of the Prairie School of architects and said:

"A pretty story could be written descriptive of the early struggles and aspirations and ultimate success of the little band of enthusiasts who had raised their standard of revolt against the disciplined ranks and array of custom. An ideal artistic atmosphere pervaded the colony in the old lofts of Steinway Hall. There was Perkins, Wright, Spencer, Myron Hunt, George Dean, Birch Long, and with them-associated in spirit if not in person-was the gifted but irresponsible genius Harvey Ellis, poet-architect, whose pencil Death stopped ere it had traced

more than a few soft lines of his dream of beauty." (*Architectural Review,* 1908)

Ellis' designs continued to influence Gustav Stickley. Although inlaid furniture was only produced for about a year between 1903 and 1904, the arches and other subtle changes to proportion were kept and used in future designs of furniture.

The years between 1904 and 1910 have been referred to as the "mature period" of Gustav Stickley. His designs incorporated the ideas of Ellis and standardization of pieces to conform to production costs. He made four finishes available "nut-brown, light brown, light brownish green, and dark brown with a tinge of gray". In 1903, Gustav introduces spindle furniture which have a lighter appearance than the box like effect of slats. He also moved to New York City and opened his new showrooms and publishing offices at 29 West Thirty-fourth Street. In 1908, he purchased land in Morris Plains, New Jersey where he hoped to build a cooperative community base upon Arts and Crafts ideals. He built a clubhouse which was modified into a home for his family who moved there in 1910. In 1913, Gustav opened a new headquarters in New York, a twelve story building with showrooms, lecture halls, and restaurant.

The years between 1913 and 1916 would be a declining period for Gustav Stickley. His furniture designs became monotonous and he dramatically cut back on structural forms to accommodate new tastes of the general public. The new Craftsman Building was a financial burden and sales in showrooms across the country were declining. On March 23, 1915, Gustav Stickley would file a petition of bankruptcy.

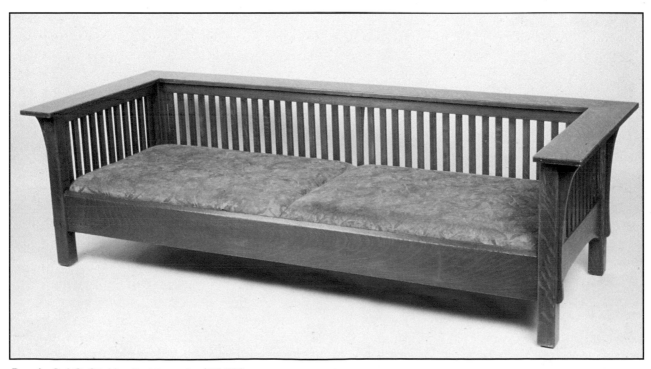

Rare L. & J.G. Stickley Prairie settle, $20,000+.

L. & J.G. Stickley, Fayetteville, New York, (c.1902 to 1924)

One of the reasons that Gustav Stickley's sales declined was due to the competition of his own brothers. His younger brother Leopold was Gustav's foreman while he was making furniture for the Tobey Furniture Company of Chicago. When Gustav severed his relationship with Tobey, Leopold with the help of a loan from Gustav, purchased a factory in Fayetteville, New York to produce furniture under contract with Tobey. Leopold made furniture for a variety of companies until 1904 when he introduced his own furniture lines under the name Onondaga Shops. Onondaga was the name of the county that the Fayetteville company was located. Another brother John George Stickley had returned East to be married. J. George Stickley had been working for another brother Albert in Michigan. Leopold persuaded J. George Stickley to stay on with him. The name of the company was changed to L. & J.G. Stickley in 1904. By 1906, the name was again changed to Handcraft.

Many of the works of L. & J.G. Stickley are quite similar to there brother Gustav's furniture. They incorporated structural details as decoration such as corbels, pegs, mortise and tenons and the use of quartered oak. In some cases the pieces reflect an English Arts and Crafts influence with feet ending in a shoe style foot. The use of machinery and the "scientific manner" were at the heart of L. & J.G. Stickley's production philosophy. The foreword of the c.1914 catalogue states:

"How your furniture is built is a matter of vital importance to you. Furniture of simple and good construction does not go out of style in a few years, but lasts your lifetime. The Work of L. & J.G. Stickley, built in a scientific manner, does not attempt to follow the traditions of a bygone day. All the resources of modern invention are used as helps in constructing this thoroughly modern product, more suitable, as many notable authorities believe, to the house of today - your house, that is - than is the furniture of past centuries or its necessarily machine made reproductions."

L. & J.G. Stickley's most modern designs were those based upon the Prairie School of design. The Prairie School of design was a Mid-Western manifestation of the Arts and Crafts Movement that emphasized the unity of the interior and exterior of architecture. There most eloquent speaker was Frank Lloyd Wright who gave an inspirational lecture at the Hull House in Chicago entitled "The Art and Craft of the Machine". In this lecture he calls the machine:

"the metamorphosis of ancient art and craft...the modern Sphinx-whose riddle the art-

ist must solve if he would that art live - for his nature holds the key."

This states the main difference between the English and American concepts of the Arts and Crafts Movement. England viewed the machine age as a dehumanizing tool whereas their American counterparts viewed the machine age as the opportunity to relieve people from monotonous labor and provide more time to create finer objects. The Prairie School designers created houses based upon simple geometric forms that emphasized the horizontal plane. At the time, there were no furnishings that were simple enough to harmonize with this new type of architecture. Wright recounted in his autobiography that:

"Very few of the houses were...anything but painful to me after the clients moved in and, helplessly, dragged the horrors of the old order along after them." (Wright, Frank Lloyd, *An Autobiography.*)

In 1912, L. & J.G. Stickley changed there name from Handcraft to The Work of L. & J.G. Stickley.

In a catalogue produced that year, L. & J.G. Stickley introduced their spindled Prairie settles. These were quite different from any of the designs of Gustav Stickley. These designs may have been greatly influenced by Peter Hansen who joined the firm in 1909. Hansen was a German born cabinet maker who worked for Gustav Stickley and became the chief designer for L. & J.G. Stickley. His wife Ruth Ann Williams was a Chicago trained draftsperson.

Stickley Brothers writing desk, $1500.

In 1915 Gustav Stickley's business had gone into bankruptcy. Leopold attempted to help his brother by creating the Stickley Associated Cabinetmakers in 1917 in which Gustav was made vice-president. The new venture was short lived and by 1916 public tastes had changed so much that L.& J.G. Stickley began to introduce a line of furniture based upon colonial revival designs. John George would die in 1921 and the last catalogue containing mission furniture was in 1922. By 1924, L. & J.G. Stickley was producing only colonial revival furniture named "Cherry Valley".

Albert Stickley, Stickley Brothers, Grand Rapids, Michigan (c.1891 to 1940).

Before John George Stickley had left his brother Albert Stickley, he had helped Albert establish the Stickley Brothers Company in 1891 in Grand Rapids, Michigan taking the name from the original company the three brothers: Gustav, Albert and Charles had started in New York. When Gustav left the original firm, Charles and Albert Stickley purchased the remaining shares. Charles would continue the company as the Stickley and Brandt Company while Albert left for Michigan.

Of all the Stickley Brothers, Albert's designs were the most influenced by Scottish and English design. His company establish a factory and showroom in London from 1897 to 1902. Albert called his version of mission furniture "Quaint" and described its origins as:

"It is to a widely different quarter of the globe that the new Quaint style owes its origin, namely Scotland. The ideals of William Morris and Burne-Jones, both Scots by blood, have been handed down and followed with an ever-widening influence, fostered and blended with the ideas of modern artists and bodies of artists, formed into societies such as the Guilded Crafts Of Scotland and the Arts and Crafts of London, to further modern artistic conceptions-exemplified in Quaint."

The Stickley Brothers furniture that Albert designed is more decorative than his brothers' furniture. Designs included inlay of various woods and metal, tapering legs, carving, curving boards and elaborate metalwork. While not all of the designs are successful in that they tend to be over elaborate or oddly proportioned, Stickley Brothers furniture presents a unique expression of British Arts and Crafts influences. J. Taylor, a leading designer and critic in Glasgow, Scotland, stated:

"If I were asked to describe them [Stickley Brothers furnishings] in a sentence I would say, *they are interesting, unconventional and artistic.*"

Charles Stickley, Stickley and Brandt Chair Company, Binghamton, New York, (c.1891 - 1919).

Charles Stickley stayed with his uncle Schuyler Brandt after his brothers went on their own. The company still produced colonial revival furniture and added a line of mission furniture. Charles' designs for mission furniture incorporated pegs and through tenons but also made use of fake tenons which sometimes protrude from joints that obviously cannot be real. Charles Stickley was truly a furniture maker and salesman. He was not professing a way of living life but simply selling furniture. The Stickley and Brandt Company declared bankruptcy in 1919.

Charles Stickley living room set, chair $500, rocker $500 and uneven arm settle $1500.

Charles P. Limbert,
Limberts Arts and Crafts Furniture,
Grand Rapids & Holland, Michigan, (c.1894 - 1944)

Charles P. Limbert would begin his furniture career as a salesman for various furniture companies including John A. Colby & Company which had also employed Gustav Stickley's associate George F. Clingman of Tobey Furniture. In 1889, Limbert became partners with Philip J. Klingman and moved to Grand Rapids, Michigan. They opened up a showroom and leased showroom space to other furniture exhibitors. The idea was a success and soon they produced a line of chairs together. By 1894, Charles P. Limbert began his own manufacturing firm. He also was the salesman for the Old Hickory Company, Martinsville, Indiana which produced furniture with the natural bark still on the wood. By 1906, Limbert moved his offices and factory to Holland, Michigan. Limbert would use as his sales pitch that concept that:

"all furniture styles, with the exception of those that are purely French, from the beginning of the 16th century down through the Flemish Renaissance (1507), the Elizabethan Renaissance (1558-1603), the Jacobean influence (1603-1649), the times of William and Mary, and Queen Anne, and the Georgian transition, (1689-1820), on even into the best of the modern schools, can be traced and their origin found in or connected with the Netherlands or the work of the Holland Dutch.

Limbert would use a brand mark on each of his pieces of furniture to authenticate them as an original creation of his Dutch workers. Limbert's furniture shows the influences of many styles. Some early bookcases are found with inlay reminiscent of Harvey Ellis's work. The most successful designs of furniture for Limbert were those based upon the Scottish School.

Charles Rennie Mackintosh (1869 - 1928) is the most well known of the Scottish School of designers. His works received praise at exhibitions in Vienna, Dresden, Moscow and Berlin. His designs contained Japanese influences and architectural utility. His famous Willow Tea Rooms in 1903 display a slant front café chair which Limbert copied almost exactly. Mackintosh's designs were published in many of the leading international design journals of the times such as *Deutsche Kunst und Dekoration*. Other designs by Limbert such as his oval tables and plant stands incorporated the square cut-outs used in Mackintosh's furniture.

By 1916, public taste is changing and Limbert begins changing its designs. Limbert introduces various styles of furniture into his catalogues to combat the slumping sales in mission furniture. In 1921, Charles Limbert would have a stroke while on a trip to Hawaii and in 1922 sold his stock in the company. He left behind a financially strong firm that would continue to produce furniture until 1944.

Limbert double oval table, (Skinner), $8000+.

Elbert Hubbard,
The Roycroft Shops,
East Aurora, New York, (1895 - 1938)

Elbert Hubbard was a great salesman and promoter. In 1892, he left a successful career with the Larkin Soap Company which produced furniture and sold his stock for $75,000. He used the money to embark upon a trip to Europe on which he met William Morris. Inspired by the ideals of the English Arts and Crafts Movement and the fine books of William Morris' Kelmscott Press, Hubbard set up a press in East Aurora, New York and named it after two seventeenth century English printers Thomas and Samuel Roycroft. He adopted the orb mark of a fourteenth century monk and combined it with the R of Roycroft. He published *Little Journeys* and *The Philistine* which were widely popular. As his publications grew he continued to add to the shops

creating a leather shop, print shop, book bindery and an inn for visitors. The furniture inspired by the inns furnishings were offered for sale by 1897. Small bookshelves were offered as premiums to customers who purchased complete sets of *Little Journeys*. A sales technique often used at the Larkin Soap Company.

Roycroft furniture is interesting in that it was an afterthought of an arts and crafts enterprise. The design of Roycroft furniture is bold and massive. Every piece was adorned with the orb mark in an obvious place in order to assure free advertising in the homes of his customers. Roycroft produced all aspects of interior furnishings and tourist items such as leather purses and copper jewelry. One of Roycroft's largest commissions

Roycroft orb mark.

Roycroft "Little Journeys" stand, $875.

Roycroft chair designed for the Grove Park Inn,
Asheville, North Carolina. (JMW Gallery), $3000.

was for the Grove Park Inn in Asheville, North Carolina. The inn was furnished with Roycroft furniture in the public rooms and large copper chandeliers designed for the natural stone lobby.

The Roycroft Shops experienced the same decline in interest by the public as other furniture manufacturers. Elbert Hubbard died aboard the Lusitania in 1915. His son kept the business intact until it went bankrupt in 1938.

J.M. Young,
J.M. Young & Sons Furniture Company,
Camden, New York, (c.1872 to 1940).

The J.M. Young Furniture Company began as early as 1872 producing a general line of Victorian furniture. It was a small family run company that had less than twenty employees. By 1904, Young offered a range of mission furniture designs based on the works of Gustav and L. & J.G. Stickley. The construction of the furniture included well done five part posts on settles and poorly added through tenons on Morris chairs. Overall J.M Young's furniture may not be as exciting in design as its competitors but has lasted due to its quality of construction.

J.M. Young Morris chair, $3000.

Rare J.M. Young rocking chair, $750.

Detail of the wavy arms used by the Harden Furniture Company.

Frank S. Harden,
Frank S. Harden Company,
McConnellsville, New York, (c.1895 - 1926).

The Frank S. Harden Company was similar to J.M. Young. A relatively small company that produced a variety of furniture including a mission furniture line. One of their most successful designs were chairs and settees with curved arms. A good example of how companies copied the designs of Gustav Stickley is exhibited in this V-back chair. Harden copies everything including the pegged corbels between the arm and leg. The only variation is in the arraignment of the stretchers.

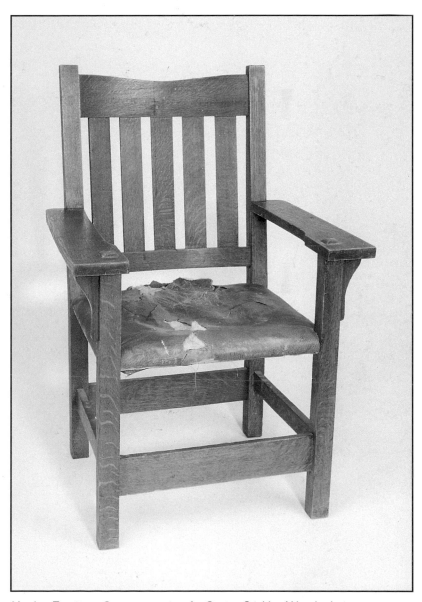

Label found on bottom of Harden chair.

Harden Furniture Company copy of a Gustav Stickley V-back chair.

Gustav Stickley V-back chairs, armchair $750, side chair $500.

John Plail,
Plail Brothers,
Wayland, New York, (c.1902 - 1933)

John Plail had worked for the Binghamton Chair Company of Binghamton, New York. In 1902, he left the firm with several other employees and created the W.H. Gunlocke Chair Company. After a few years, Plail and his brother Joseph left the firm and created Plail Brothers Chair Company. The most successful design of this firm was their selection of barrel form furniture.

These designs were probably influenced by the bent wood forms of the Austrian firm of Jacob and Josef Kohn. In 1914 the company would burn to the ground. John Plail rebuilt but by then tastes were changing. The company introduced lines that appealed to the public and managed to stay in business until the depression. The company closed in 1933.

A.A. Barber,
Grand Rapids Bookcase andChair Company,
Hastings, Michigan, (c.1911 - ?).

Lifetime Furniture was the creation of two companies that merged in 1911. The Grand Rapids Bookcase Company and the Barber Brothers Chair Company united to combine the lines of mission furniture each company was already making. The companies were also located on adjoining land make it a fiscally good decision. The new furniture was called "Cloister Furniture" harking back to medieval England. Lifetime furniture used construction techniques which made the furniture cheaper and more accessible to people. For instance, a single piece of glass was used behind applied mullions that gave the appearance of individual panes of glass. Overall Lifetime made good quality mission furniture with nice selections of quartered oak.

Lifetime hall bench, $1100.

C.C. Brooks,
Brooks Manufacturing Company,
Saginaw, Michigan, (c.1901 - 1922)

The Brooks Manufacturing Company began as boat maker and entered into the furniture business around 1909. Brooks' furniture designs were copies of his predecessors. Brooks specialized in furniture that could be shipped in parts and placed together by the customer. The Brooks 1912 catalogue states:

> "Buying goods by mail, heretofore generally misunderstood but now better recognized as 'Modern Purchasing' offers, beyond a question of a doubt the greatest opportunity for money saving in the business world today."

By 1915 sales would begin to decline and in 1922 the Brooks Manufacturing Company declared bankruptcy.

Brooks Furniture Company screen, $500.

Oscar F. Onken,
The Shop of the Crafters,
Cincinnati, Ohio, (c.1904 - 1931).

In 1880 Oscar F. Onken, at the age of 22, began as a picture frame maker. He became a retailer in 1893 and began the production of furniture in 1905. He hired Paul Horti who inspired many of Onken's designs. The Shop of the Crafters catalogue introduction states:

"Professor Horti's dining room at the St. Louis Fair and his designs for the decoration of the Hungarian sections in the Palace of Fine Arts Building, Manufacturer's Building and Mines and Metallurgy Building were so wholly delightful in their originality as to have exerted a far reaching influence on the general crafts' movement. His work with the Shop of the Crafters of Cincinnati has contributed to the distinction it enjoys for productions that are pure in style and of artistic beauty."

The designs of the Shop of the Crafters were Austrian in inspiration and Onken promoted the Secessionist style in his furniture catalogues. These designs included elaborate veneered woods and bold decorative forms with cut-outs. The company is believed to have stopped producing furniture around 1920.

Rare Shop of the Crafters book cases, $3000 each.

William Leavens,
William Leavens & Company,
Boston, Massachusetts, (c.1896 - 1947).

The William Leavens company was located at 32 Canal Street and 31 Merrimac Street in Boston, Massachusetts. The company produced colonial revival furniture and introduced a line called "Cottage Furniture" which included "Dutch" furniture designs. Leavens prided itself on being able to cater to the needs of its customers stating:

"We claim to be the sole makers and finishers of this style of Cottage furniture, and our shop is the only one in the country where the finish is at the command of the buyer."

At its best, Leavens designs reflect those of Limbert or Gustav Stickley. It is interesting to note that Leavens retailed Old Hickory Furniture that Limbert had once worked for. But most designs lack a structural emphasis and leave the furniture somewhat plain. The company continued to produce colonial revival furniture along with its Cottage line and finally closed in 1947.

No. 1037
DUTCH RECLINING ROCKER
Solid Quartered Oak, any finish. Weight, frame, 50 lbs.
Cushion, 23 lbs.   Price of frame, $18.00.   Cushions
in Denim and Burlap, all hair, $9.00. Cotton, $6.75.
Cushions, Span. Roan Leather, welted, cotton, $16.50.
"   "   "   "   "   "   hair,   21.00.
Lacing, extra, per set, $1.50.

No. 1038
DUTCH RECLINING CHAIR
Solid Quartered Oak, any finish.   Weight, 46 lbs.
Cushion, 23 lbs. Price of frame, $15.00. Cushions
in Denim or Burlap, all hair, $9.00. Cotton, $6.75.
Cushions, Span. Roan Leather, welted cotton, $16.50.
"   "   "   "   "   "   hair, 21.00.
Lacing, extra, per set, $1.50.

WILLIAM LEAVENS & CO., Manufacturers, Boston, Mass.

William Leavens Dutch furniture, rocker and chair $1200 each.

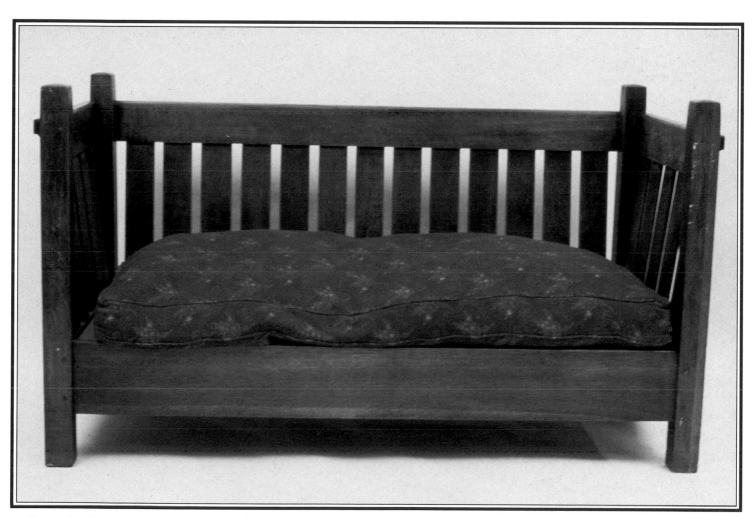

Gustav Stickley settle, ht. 39", wd. 68", d. 33-1/2", (Skinner), $10,000.

Gustav Stickley spindle back settle, #290, branded
mark, ht. 31", wd. 49-1/2", d. 27-3/4", $10,000.

L. & J.G. Stickley
hall settle, #209,
signed "The Work
of...", $4000.

L. & J.G. Stickley settle, #229, unsigned,
ht. 36", wd. 72", d. 26", $10,000.

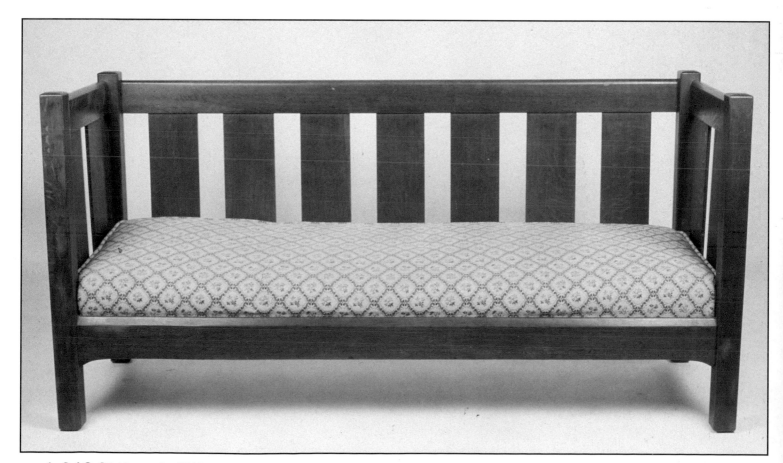

L. & J.G. Stickley settle, #216,
ht. 36", wd. 72", d. 26", $5000.

Plail Brothers barrel form furniture, settle ht.
33-1/2", wd. 46-1/4"", $8000, chair, $3000.

L. & J.G. Stickley Prairie settle, #220, signed "The Work of...", ht. 29", wd. 84-1/2", d. 36-3/4", (Skinner), $30,000.

Gustav Stickley settee, #214, $7000, matching arm chair $3000.

Gustav Stickley settle, 222, ht. 36", wd. 80", $15,000+.

Stickley Brothers hall settee, #3315, $2500.

Gustav Stickley mahogany hall settee,
ht. 31-1/2", wd. 53-1/4", d. 20-1/2", $3000.

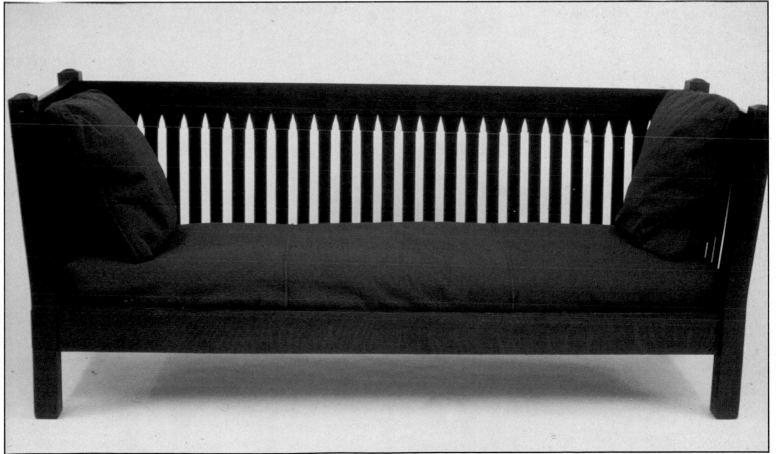

Stickley Brothers settle, #905-3865, ht. 36", wd. 84", d. 29-1/2", $8000.

L. & J.G. Stickley spindle settle, #234, $7000.

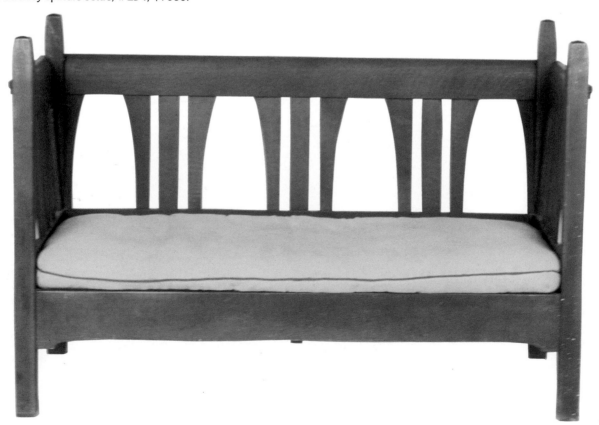

Gustav Stickley settee, (Skinner), $10,000.

Arts and Crafts settee with leather upholstery, $4000.

Harden Furniture Company settle,
$2500, matching chair $750.

Stickley Brothers hall
settee, #3578, ht. 36",
wd. 40", d. 19", $750.

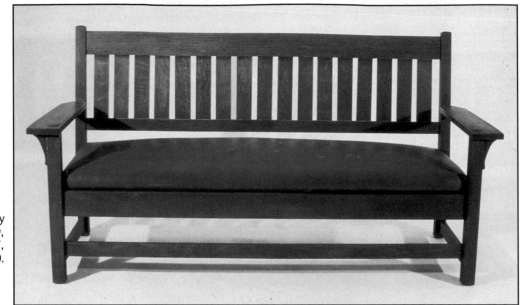

Gustav Stickley
settle, #219,
ht. 39", wd. 72",
d. 23", $2500.

Charles Stickley drop
arm settle, ht. 40-1/2",
wd. 72", $1200.

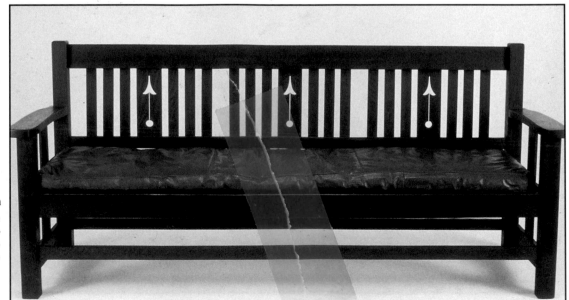

Limbert settle with
spade cut-outs,
#507, ht. 35-1/2",
wd. 76-3/4",
d. 25-1/2", $3500.

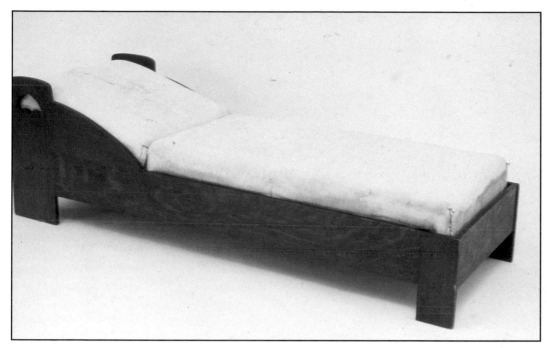

Limbert daybed,
#651, $3500.

Limbert settle,
#829, ht. 36", wd.
69", d. 24", $1500.

L. & J.G. Stickley pull out bed, branded "The Work of...", $8000+.

L. & J.G. Stickley settee, #225, ht. 36-3/4", wd. 52-1/2", $2200.

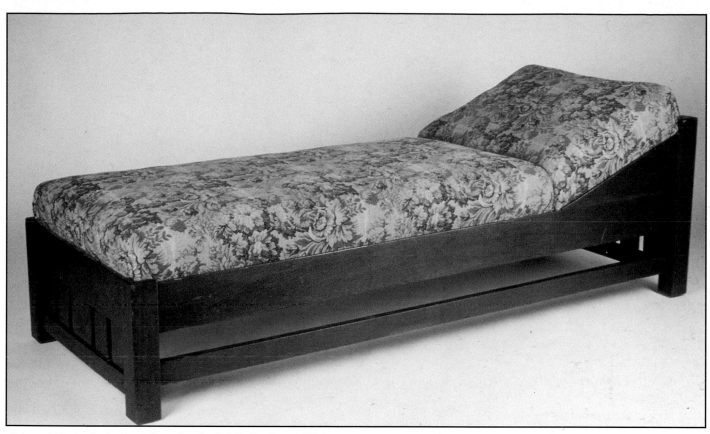

Arts and Crafts daybed, attributed to L. & J.G. Stickley, $2500.

Gustav Stickley hall seat, $8000.

Rockers and Chairs

Gustav Stickley arm rocker, #323, $2500.

L. & J.G. Stickley rocker on left $1200, rocker on right $650.

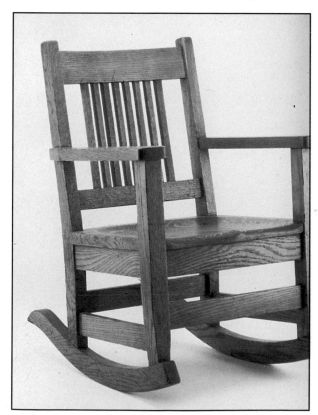

Child's spindle rocker, maker unknown, $250.

Gustav Stickley child's rocker, $300.

Gustav Stickley child's arm rocker,
#345, ht. 25-1/2", wd. 18", $500.

Arts and Crafts style wicker
rocker with broad arms, $500.

Limbert arm rocker, #819, brand mark, ht. 32-1/2", wd. 32", d. 32", $3500.

Gustav Stickley
rocker, #387,
$600.

L. & J.G. Stickley arm
rocker, #837, signed
"The Work of...", $1200.

Above:
L. & J.G. Stickley rocking
Morris chair, #831, $2500.

Right:
L. & J.G. Stickley rocker,
$950.

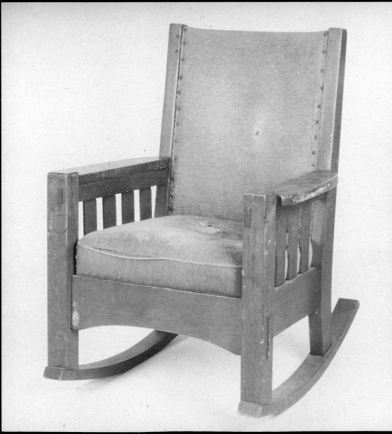

Above:
Limbert rocker with ebony inlay, $1500.

Left:
Arts and Crafts rocker attributed to Harden, $500.

Roycroft chairs, $1000 each.

Joseph P. McHugh dining chair, $500.

Gustav Stickley inlaid side chair, $5000+.

Gustav Stickley
inlaid arm chair
designed by
Harvey Ellis,
ht. 47-3/4",
wd. 18-1/2",
d. 15-1/2",
(Skinner),
$25,000+.

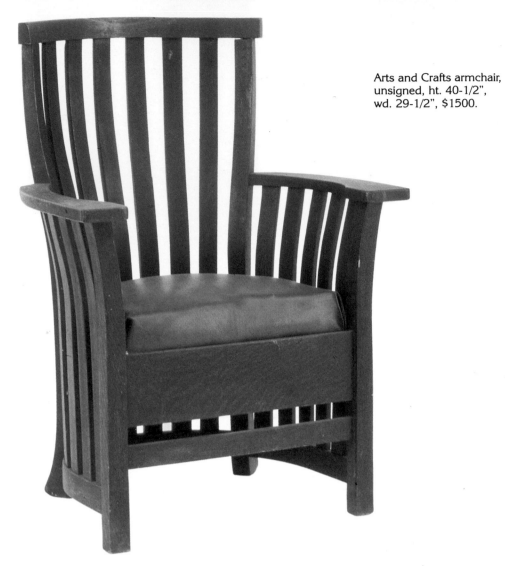

Arts and Crafts armchair,
unsigned, ht. 40-1/2",
wd. 29-1/2", $1500.

Gustav Stickley armchair, unsigned,
ht. 38-3/4", wd. 31-1/2", d. 29", $1500.

Gustav Stickley armchair, ht. 37", wd. 27", $1500.

Stickley Brothers
armchair, Quaint
decal, $1500.

Arts and Crafts armchair attributed to
Karpen, Chicago, ht. 35", wd. 29", $1200.

Arts and Crafts armchair, ht. 26-1/4", wd. 28-1/2", $300.

Left:
Brooks Company
spindle chair, #4, ht.
33", wd. 36", d. 30-1/2",
$2000.

Below:
Gustav Stickley spindle
chair, #391, unsigned,
ht. 29", wd. 25-1/4",
d. 28", $8000.

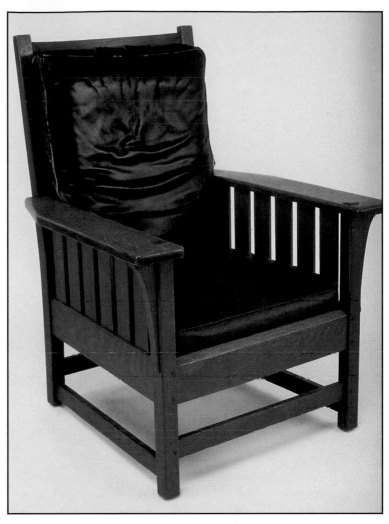

Right:
L. & J.G. Stickley armchair, #448, signed "The Work of...", $2000.

Below:
Gustav Stickley chair, #331, ht. 29", wd. 25-1/4", d. 27-3/4", $5000.

L. & J.G. Stickley armchairs, #836,
ht. 47", wd. 28", d. 19-1/2", $1200 each.

Arts and Crafts armchair with inlay, $1200.

L. & J.G. Stickley armchair, #408, $3000.

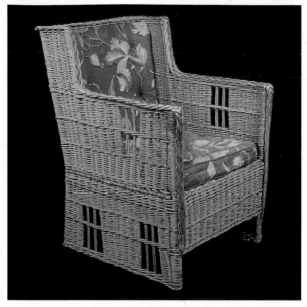

Gustav Stickley
Willow wicker chair,
#85, $2500.

Gustav Stickley
bow-arm Morris
chair, #2340, ht.
38", wd. 28-1/4", d.
32-1/2",(Skinner),
$10,000+.

Gustav Stickley Morris chair, #332, unsigned, ht. 38", wd. 28-1/4", d. 32-1/2", $8000+.

Gustav Stickley drop-arm Morris chair, #369, ht. 36", wd. 33", d. 38", $10,000+.

Gustav Stickley spindle Morris chair, #369, unsigned,
ht. 37-1/4", wd. 33", d. 28", (Skinner), $12,000+.

L. & J.G. Stickley open-arm Morris chair, #830, $1000.

Stickley Brothers Morris chair, $2500.

Roycroft Morris chair, $7000.

Gustav Stickley Morris chair, #332, $8000+.

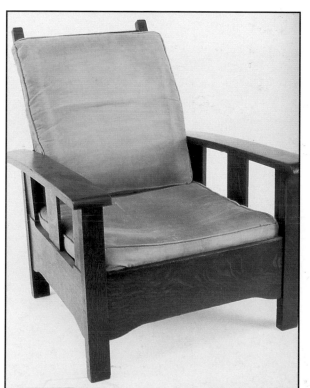

Arts and Crafts Morris chair with broad slats, unsigned, $2000.

Gustav Stickley
spindle Morris chair,
#367, $10,000+.

Limbert Morris chair,
#521, ht. 37-1/2",
wd. 34", d. 42",
$8000+.

L. & J.G. Stickley
Morris chair,
#471, $3000.

Gustav Stickley
bow-arm Morris
chair, $10,000+.

Gustav Stickley Morris chair, $8000+.

L. & J.G. Stickley open-arm Morris chair, $1000.

Arts and Crafts Morris chair, $1200.

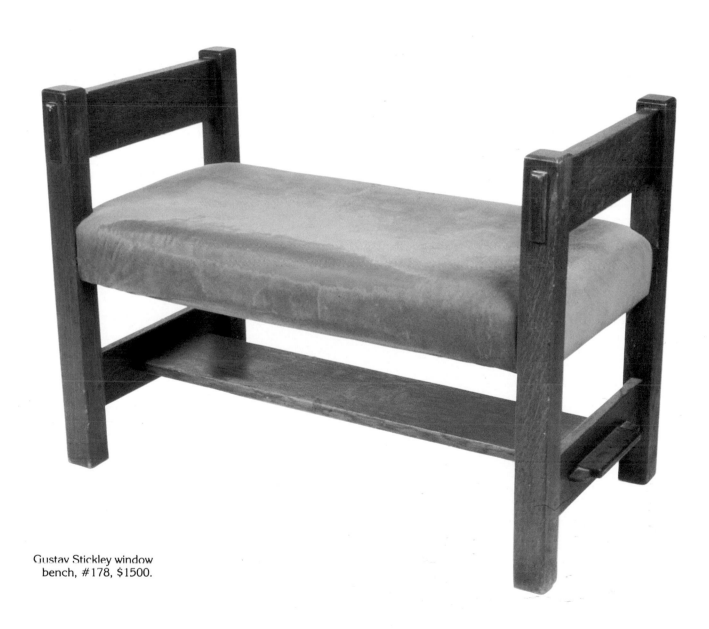

Gustav Stickley window
bench, #178, $1500.

Gustav Stickley bench, #217, ht. 21", wd. 36", d. 13", $1200.

Derby & Company window seat, ht. 28", wd. 22", d. 14", $500.

Stickley Brothers footstool, ht. 28", wd. 22", d. 14", $650.

Gustav Stickley footstool, #726, ht. 5", wd. 13", $600.

Gustav Stickley spindle footstool,
ht. 15", wd. 20-1/2", d. 16", $1500.

Gustav Stickley Eastwood footstool, #725,
ht. 15", wd. 20", d. 16", (Skinner), $5000.

Arts and Crafts footstool attributed to Harden, $650.

J.M. Young footstool, $475.

Arts and Crafts window bench
attributed to J.M. Young, $600.

Gustav Stickley
footstool, $400.

Gustav Stickley small directors table, branded mark,
ht. 30", wd. 54", d. 31-1/2", (Skinner), $10,000+.

Limbert console table, #1112, ht. 29", wd. 66", d. 21", $5000.

Gustav Stickley child's bench, $1500,
child's trestle table, #639, $1500.

Limbert table, #120, ht. 29", diameter 45", $4000.

Above:
Stickley Brothers lamp table, ht. 29",
diameter 28-1/2", $1500.

Left:
Arts and Crafts chair table, $1200.

Gustav Stickley directors table, #631,
ht. 29-1/2", wd. 96-1/2", d. 48", $15,000+.

Gustav Stickley table, #626, ht. 30", diameter 40", $3500.

Gustav Stickley table, #439, ht. 28", d. 30", $3500.

Gustav Stickley table with stacking stretchers, #624, $7500+.

Gustav Stickley library table, #636, ht. 29", diameter 48", $5000+.

Gustav Stickley table with leather top, #441, ht. 30", diameter 36", $3500.

L. & J.G. Stickley table, #580, ht. 29-1/4", wd. 36", $2500.

Arts and Crafts plant stand, $250.

Gustav Stickley table, #609, ht. 29", diameter 36", $2500.

Arts and Crafts table attributed
to Gustav Stickley , $1500.

L. & J.G. Stickley plant stand, $1500.

Gustav Stickley plant stand, $1500.

Limbert oval table, $3500.

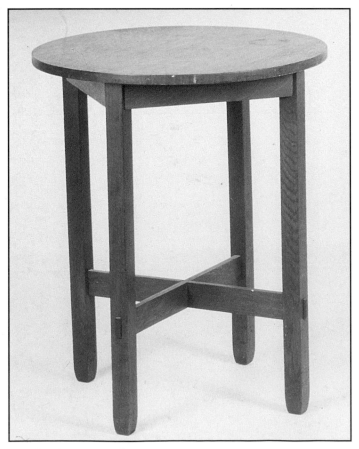

Limbert lamp table, $750.

Arts and Crafts plant stand, $250.

Arts and Crafts plant stand with cut-outs, $250.

Stickley Brothers plant stand, ht. 34", wd. 14", $1500.

Roycroft tabouret, ht. 19", wd. 12", $1500+.

Limbert plant stand, #240,
ht. 30", wd. 20", $4000+.

Limbert plant stand, $2500+.

Limbert stand, #751,
ht. 36", wd. 24-3/4",
d. 17", $2500.

Gustav Stickley stand, #618, $4000.

Arts and Crafts stand with strap hinges, possibly English, $500.

Gustav Stickley stand, #89, $4000+.

Arts and Crafts stand, unsigned, $2000.

Stickley Brothers stand, ht. 34", wd. 18", $1800.

Arts and Crafts stand, $2000.

Arts and Crafts stand, $2000.

Roycroft magazine stand, #22, ht. 30", wd. 26", d. 15", $2500.

Roycroft bookshelf, #87, ht. 38-1/2", wd. 32-1/2", d. 15-1/2", $5000+.

Limbert magazine stand, #346,
ht. 40", wd. 24", d. 14", $3000.

Roycroft magazine stand,
#78, ht. 37", wd. 18", $2000.

L. & J.G. Stickley
book table, #516, ht.
28-1/4", wd. 26-1/4",
d. 26-1/4", $5000+.

Roycroft magazine
stand, $5000+.

Arts and Crafts spindle bookcase
attributed to Stickley Brothers, $1500.

Opposite page left:
L. & J.G. Stickley magazine
stand, #45, ht. 42", wd. 21",
d. 12", $1800.

Opposite page right:
Limbert magazine stand, ht.
37", wd. 16", d. 13", $2000.

Gustav Stickley folio stand,
#551, ht. 40-1/2", wd. 29-3/4",
d. 12", $3000+.

Gustav Stickley
bookrack, $1800.

Arts and Crafts magazine stand, $500.

Arts and Crafts magazine stand, $1200.

Arts and Crafts magazine stand, $750.

Gustav Stickley spindle-side library table, (Skinner), $6000+.

L. & J.G. Stickley mouse
hole library table, $3500+.

Limbert two drawer library table, $2500.

Limbert library table, ht. 30", wd. 44", d. 30", $1500.

Roycroft library table, $3000.

Limbert table with square cut-outs, $4000.

Gustav Stickley three drawer
spindle-side library table, $7000+.

Stickley Brothers
library table,
$2500.

Gustav Stickley spindle table, $5000+.

Arts and Crafts
library table
attributed to Gustav
Stickley, $1500.

Desks and Items for the Study

Gustav Stickley desk, (Skinner), $10,000+.

Interior of Gustav Stickley desk.

L. & J.G. Stickley desk with book shelves, $2000.

Roycroft slant front desk, $2000.

Gustav Stickley swivel office chair, $3000.

Gustav Stickley wastepaper basket, $800.

Gustav Stickley fall
front desk, $2500.

Interior of Gustav
Stickley desk.

Gustav Stickley fall front
desk, #552, ht. 48-1/4",
wd. 32-3/4", d. 14",
(Skinner), $10,000+.

Gustav Stickley postcard desk, $2500.

Interior of Gustav
Stickley desk.

Gustav Stickley desk with letter box top, $3000.

Gustav Stickley desk, $3000.

Arts and Crafts desk with book shelf sides, $450.

Stickley Brothers fall front desk, $2500.

Gustav Stickley
music cabinet,
#70, amber glass
panes, ht. 47-1/4",
wd. 19-1/4",
d. 16", (Skinner),
$10,000.

Gustav Stickley open
bookcase, ht. 56",
wd. 62", d. 12-1/2",
$6000.

Gustav Stickley open bookcase,
ht. 56", wd. 36", $4000.

L. & J.G. Stickley bookcase, #652,
signed "The Work of...", $2000.

Limbert triple door bookcase, $6000.

Arts and Crafts two door bookcase, $4000.

Above:
L. & J.G. Stickley three door bookcase, #331, ht. 56", wd. 70", d. 12", (Skinner), $7000+.

Left:
Arts and Crafts bookcase, unsigned, $700.

L. & J.G. Stickley double door bookcase with keys and tenons, $4000+.

Arts and Crafts bookcase attributed to Charles Stickley, $3000.

Left:
Gustav Stickley bookcase,
#512, ht. 60-1/2", wd. 28",
d. 10-1/4", $8000+.

L. & J.G. Stickley single
door bookcase, $4000+.

Arts and Crafts triple
door bookcase, $1500.

Gustav Stickley
bookcase,
ht. 64-1/2",
wd. 42", d. 14",
$10,000+.

Gustav Stickley double door bookcase, $5000.

Gustav Stickley bookcase, ht. 45", wd. 36", d. 12", $4000.

Gustav Stickley bookcase, #716, ht. 55", wd. 42-3/4", d. 13", (Skinner,), $10,000.

Gustav Stickley bookcase designed by Harvey
Ellis, ht. 58", wd. 36", d. 14", $12,000+.

Lifetime bookcase, $2200.

Gustav Stickley bookcase, $4000.

Gustav Stickley
bookcase, #704,
ht. 58", wd. 60",
$12,000+.

Roycroft bookcase, #E084,
ht. 60-1/2", wd. 31-1/4",
d. 15-1/2", (Skinner),
$10,000+.

Limbert bookcase with heart cut-out,
ht. 43-1/2", wd. 24", d. 12", $5000.

Dining Tables, Dining Chairs, Sideboards, Servers and China Closets

Gustav Stickley server with butterfly jointed doors, (Skinner), $10,000+.

L. & J.G. Stickley dining table, #720, signed "The Work of...", diameter 54", $4000.

Arts and Crafts dining table, diameter 54", $800.

L. & J.G. Stickley drop leaf table, #553, ht. 30", diameter 42", $2500.

Arts and Crafts lunch table, unsigned, diameter 36-1/2", $1500.

Stickley Brothers dining
table, ht. 30-1/2",
diameter 48", $2000.

Roycroft dining table,
diameter 48", $8000+.

Gustav Stickley dining table, diameter 48", $6000+.

Gustav Stickley dining table, #634, ht. 30", diameter 54", (Skinner), $10,000.

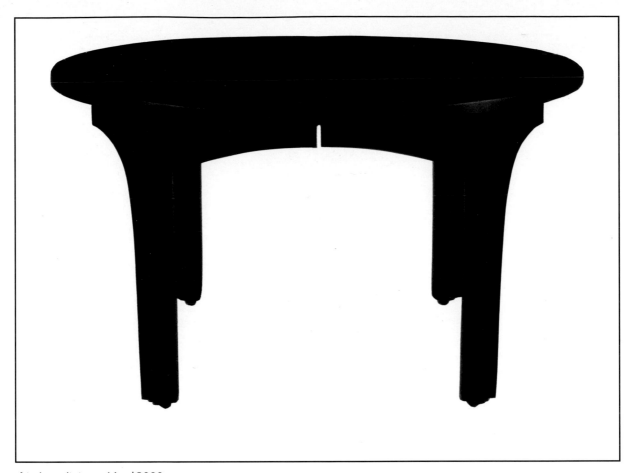

Limbert dining table, $3000.

L. & J.G. Stickley
dining table, $4000.

Gustav Stickley dining chairs, $475 each.

Gustav Stickley dining chair, #352, ht. 37-1/2", wd. 18", $500, armchair, #352A, $600.

Stickley Brothers dining table, diameter 48", $3000, dining chair $350, dining arm chair $400.

Limbert dining chairs, $400 each.

Gustav Stickley spindle dining chairs, ht. 39",
wd. 16-3/4", d. 16-1/4", $1500 each.

Gustav Stickley
spindle dining
chair, (Skinner),
$1000.

Gustav Stickley H-back dining
arm chairs $500 each.

Gustav Stickley dining chairs, $500 each.

Gustav Stickley spindle dining chair, $2000.

L. & J.G. Stickley
dining chairs,
$275 each.

Stickley Brothers dining chairs, $350 each, arm chair $400.

Gustav Stickley dining chair, $300.

L. & J.G. Stickley dining chairs, $350 each.

Gustav Stickley dining arm chair, #355a, ht. 36-1/4",
wd. 26", d. 22", $1200, dining chair $700.

Gustav Stickley spindle arm chair, $3000.

Arts and Crafts armchair attributed to Gustav Stickley, $700.

Gustav Stickley dining chairs, $500 each.

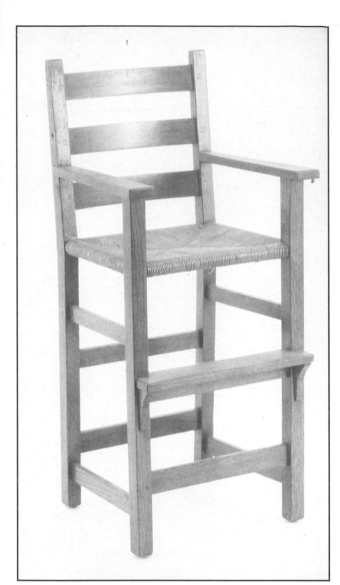

Gustav Stickley child's highchair, $1200.

L. & J.G. Stickley dining arm chair, $350, side chair, $300.

Gustav Stickley hanging plate rack, $2500+.

Gustav Stickley dinner gong, $3000+.

Limbert server,
$3500+.

Gustav Stickley server, $6000+.

Gustav Stickley
server, $4000.

L. & J.G.
Stickley server,
$4000.

Gustav Stickley server, $4000.

Arts and Crafts
china cabinet,
unsigned, $800.

Gustav Stickley
single door china
cabinet, $6000.

Gustav Stickley single door china cabinet, $5000.

Limbert china
cabinet, $5000.

Gustav Stickley single door china cabinet, (Skinner), $5000.

L. & J.G. Stickley china cabinet, $6000.

Gustav Stickley
sideboard,
$4000.

Limbert sideboard
with cut-outs, $5000.

Stickley Brothers sideboard, $1500.

Arts and Crafts sideboard with cut-out design, $2200.

L. & J.G. Stickley sideboard with plate rail, $3500.

Limbert sideboard, $7000.

Limbert sideboard with plate rail, (Skinner), $7000.

Gustav Stickley server, $7000.

Lifetime
sideboard,
$1200.

L. & J.G. Stickley sideboard with strap hinges, $4500.

L. & J.G. Stickley
sideboard with plate
rail, $2500.

L. & J.G. Stickley
sideboard, $3500.

Limbert sideboard with mirror, $3500.

Gustav Stickley sideboard with open shelf, $3500.

Limbert sideboard with
extended corbels, $6000.

Gustav Stickley sideboard, #814-1/2,
ht. 38" wd. 56", d. 22", $6500.

Lighting Fixtures

Tiffany daffodil table lamp, signed "Tiffany
Studios New York", ht. 21, (Skinner), $20,000.

Gustav Stickley desk lamp, $3000.

Gustav Stickley floor lamp with wicker shade, $4000.

Arts and Crafts copper lamp with wicker shade, $800.

Tiffany lemon leaf table lamp, signed "Tiffany Studios New York", (Skinner), $10,000.

Fulper Pottery table lamp, ht. 17", diameter 16-1/2", $20,000.

Arts and Crafts copper lamp with mica shade, unsigned, $1200.

Tiffany fleur-de-lis table lamp, (Skinner), $10,000.

Arts and Crafts chandelier, $800.

Bradley & Hubbard lamp with slag glass shade, $750.

Bradley & Hubbard lamp with reverse painted decoration, $1500.

Gustav Stickley lantern with cut-outs, $1500.

Arts and Crafts lamp with silver overlay, $2000.

152

Limbert lamp with copper and mica shade
on a oak base, #7, (Skinner), $20,000+.

Handel chandelier with frosted glass shades, $4000.

Below:
Handel lamp with cased and acid etched shade, $3000.

Below:
Handel wall sconce, $950.

Arts and Crafts chandelier with slag glass, $1200.

Arts and Crafts table lamp with slag glass shade, $400.

Miscellaneous

Gustav Stickley wardrobe, ht. 60-1/4",
wd. 34-1/4", d. 16-3/4", $10,000.

Gustav Stickley three drawer stand, #842,
ht. 29-1/2", wd. 22", d. 16", $3000.

Arts and Crafts bed, ht. 51", wd. 45-1/2", $300.

Arts and Crafts paneled bed, ht. 60-1/2", wd. 57", $800.

Gustav Stickley
dresser, #911,
ht. 66", wd. 48",
d. 22", (Skinner),
$4000.

Gustav Stickley
twin bed, ht. 46",
wd. 40", $4000.

Prairie School style bed, ht. 68", wd. 62", $2000.

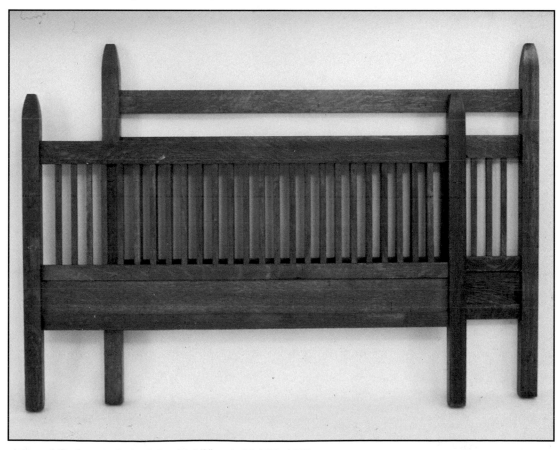

Arts and Crafts spindle bed, ht. 47-1/2", wd. 57-1/2", $800.

Gustav Stickley chest, #614, ht.
62", wd. 42", (Skinner), $12,000+.

Gustav Stickley chest,
#902, ht. 52-1/2",
$6000+.

Stickley Brothers chest,
ht. 66", wd. 44", d. 22",
$2500.

Gustav Stickley chest,
#901, ht. 44", wd. 37",
d. 19", $3000.

Gustav Stickley dresser,
#905, ht. 65-1/2", wd. 48",
d. 22-1/2", $6000+.

Opposite page:
Gustav Stickley chest,
#913, ht. 50", wd. 36",
d. 19", $10,000.

Gustav Stickley chest,
#902, ht. 52-1/2",
wd. 40", d. 21-3/4",
$5000.

Gustav Stickley bed, #923, ht. 47-1/2", wd. 45", $4000.

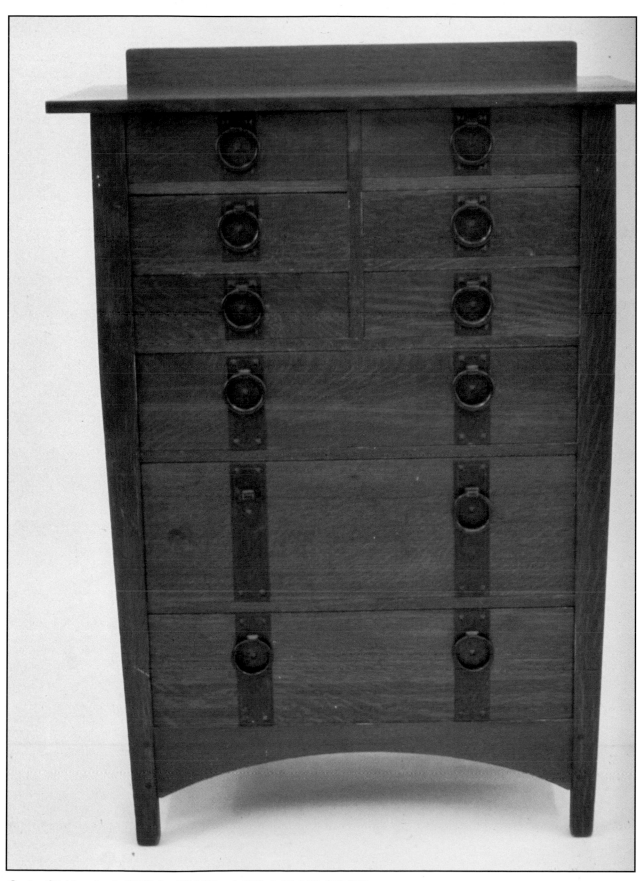

Gustav Stickley chest, #913, ht. 50-1/2", wd. 36", d. 19-1/2", $12,000.

L. & J.G. Stickley
wardrobe, (Skinner),
$10,000.

Stickley Brothers
chest, $1500.

Roycroft dressing table, ht. 56-1/4",
wd. 39", d. 17-1/2", $3000.

Roycroft chest,
$10,000.

Roycroft bridal chest, #097, $7000+.

Opposite page:
Gustav Stickley leather
covered folding screen,
ht. 69-1/2", wd. 21-3/4",
$5000+.

Gustav Stickley inlaid bed designed by
Harvey Ellis, ht. 58", wd. 59-1/2", $15,000+.

Gustav Stickley bridal chest with strap hinges, $10,000+.

Arts and Crafts blanket chest with conventionalized Chinese lily design by Ernest Batchelder, unsigned, $15,000+.

Roycroft sewing table, ht. 29", wd. 30", d. 16-1/2", $3500.

Roycroft mahogany box with copper trim, ht. 8", wd. 14", d. 12", $2000.

Roycroft "Ali Baba" bench, ht. 17", wd. 42", d. 15", $3000.

Gustav Stickley
mantel clock, ht. 21",
wd. 13-1/2", d. 8",
(Skinner), $10,000.

Roycroft six panel frame, ht. 11", wd. 37-1/2", $500.

Gustav Stickley fire screen, #104, ht. 35", wd. 31", $4000.

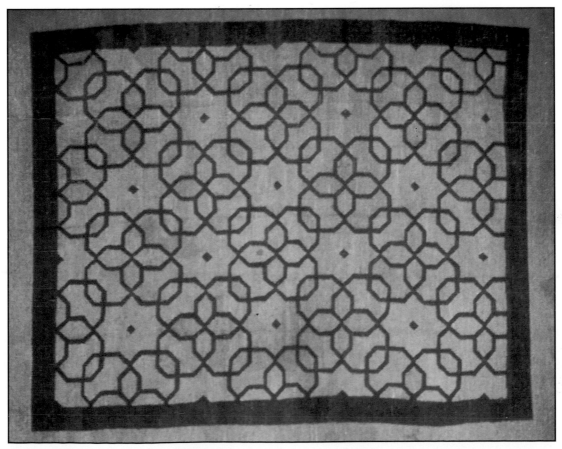

Gustav Stickley rug, 9 ft.x12 ft, $2500.

Roycroft copper tea and coffee service, $1500.

Shop of the Crafters
stand, ht. 46", wd.
14-1/2", $2000.

Gustav Stickley umbrella
stand, #100, ht. 24",
diameter 12-1/2", $1200.

Opposite page:
Gustav Stickley hall tree, ht. 74",
wd. 37-1/2", d. 13-3/4", $5000+.

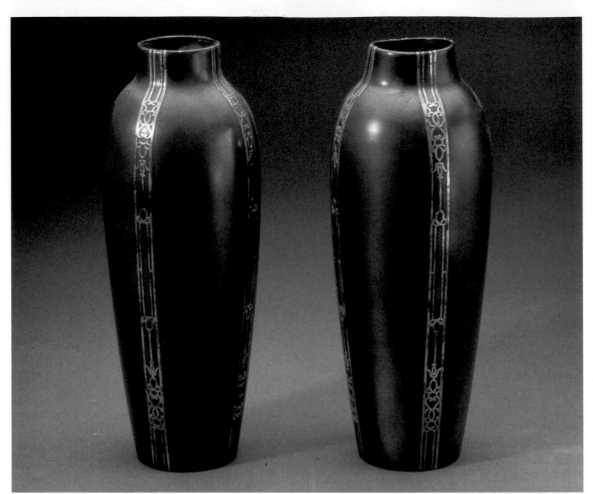

Heintz Art Metal Shop
bronze and silver
vases, ht. 11-1/4",
$600 pair.

L. & J.G. Stickley
copper jardiniere, ht. 8,
diameter 9-1/2", $800.

Roycroft copper serving tray, diameter 15-1/2", $600.

Arts and Crafts linens, $100-300 each.

William Leavens Furniture Company, Boston, Retail Plates

To Our Prospective Customers

THE increasing demand for plain, simple furniture obliges us to make the manufacturing of goods like the enclosed sketches a part of our business. People who love the **Old New England Styles** for their simplicity, will find in our Catalogue a few reproductions and many suggestions. Our specialty is Cottage Furniture, adapted to shore and country houses. This furniture is made of oak, and can be stained any color to match interior decorations, or it can be had from us in the unfinished state to be stained to suit purchaser. We claim to be the sole makers and finishers of this style of Cottage Furniture, and our shop is the only one in the country where the finish is at the command of the buyer. Our price is for goods free on board cars or express in Boston, with no charge for packing.

When ordering goods, use name and number and color of finish. If special sizes or designs are desired, rough sketches and specifications will have prompt attention.

The prices marked on the pictures are for goods stained in standard stains. We finish white or tinted enamel when desired, also in mahogany color, an additional charge of 10% being made for this work. A discount is made for unfinished goods.

William Leavens & Co.

32 Canal St., Boston

Leavens catalogue introduction.

No. 2091
COTTAGE BOOK RACK
Solid Oak, any color finish. 30 in. high, 27 in. wide, 9 in. deep.
Weight, 15 lbs. Price, $3.75.

WILLIAM LEAVENS & CO., Manufacturers,
Boston, Mass.

Leavens book rack, $100.

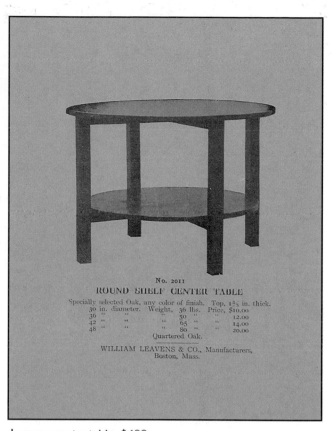

No. 2011
ROUND SHELF CENTER TABLE
Specially selected Oak, any color of finish. Top, 1⅜ in. thick.

30 in. diameter.	Weight,	36 lbs.	Price,	$10.00
36 " "	"	50 "	"	12.00
42 " "	"	65 "	"	14.00
48 " "	"	80 "	"	20.00

Quartered Oak.

WILLIAM LEAVENS & CO., Manufacturers,
Boston, Mass.

Leavens center table, $400.

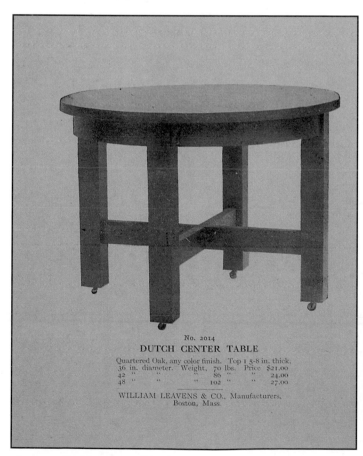

No. 2014
DUTCH CENTER TABLE
Quartered Oak, any color finish. Top 1 5-8 in. thick.

36 in. diameter.	Weight,	70 lbs.	Price	$21.00
42 " "	"	86 "	"	24.00
48 " "	"	102 "	"	27.00

WILLIAM LEAVENS & CO., Manufacturers,
Boston, Mass.

Leavens Dutch center table, $400.

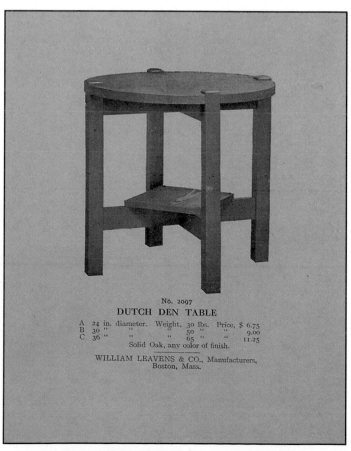

No. 2097
DUTCH DEN TABLE

A	24 in. diameter.	Weight,	30 lbs.	Price,	$ 6.75
B	30 " "	"	50 "	"	9.00
C	36 " "	"	65 "	"	11.25

Solid Oak, any color of finish.

WILLIAM LEAVENS & CO., Manufacturers,
Boston, Mass.

Leavens Dutch den table, $300.

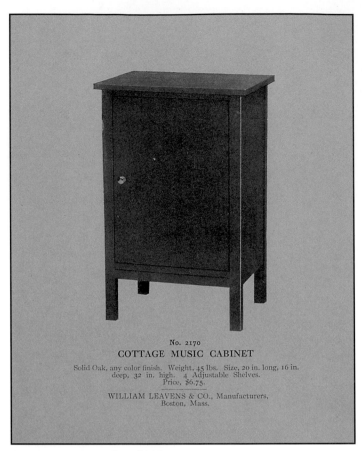

No. 2170
COTTAGE MUSIC CABINET

Solid Oak, any color finish. Weight, 45 lbs. Size, 20 in. long, 16 in. deep, 32 in. high. 4 Adjustable Shelves. Price, $6.75.

WILLIAM LEAVENS & CO., Manufacturers, Boston, Mass.

Leavens music cabinet, $200.

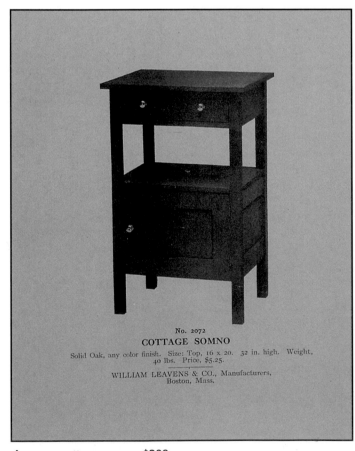

No. 2072
COTTAGE SOMNO

Solid Oak, any color finish. Size: Top, 16 x 20. 32 in. high. Weight, 40 lbs. Price, $5.25.

WILLIAM LEAVENS & CO., Manufacturers, Boston, Mass.

Leavens cottage somno, $300.

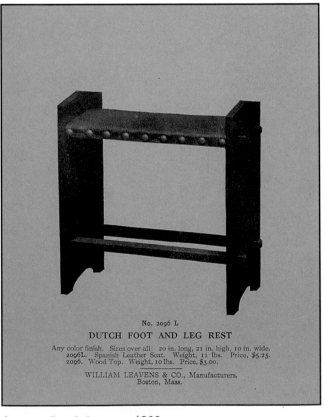

No. 2096 L
DUTCH FOOT AND LEG REST

Any color finish. Sizes over all: 20 in. long, 21 in. high, 10 in. wide. 2096L. Spanish Leather Seat. Weight, 11 lbs. Price, $5.25. 2096. Wood Top. Weight, 10 lbs. Price, $3.00.

WILLIAM LEAVENS & CO., Manufacturers, Boston, Mass.

Leavens Dutch foot rest, $200.

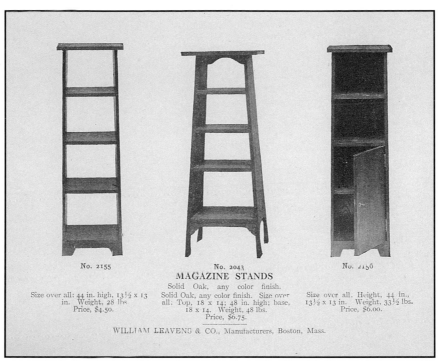

No. 2155

No. 2043
MAGAZINE STANDS
Solid Oak, any color finish.

No. 2156

Size over all: 44 in. high, 13½ x 13 in. Weight, 28 lbs. Price, $4.50.

Solid Oak, any color finish. Size over all: Top, 18 x 14; 48 in. high; base, 18 x 14. Weight, 48 lbs. Price, $6.75.

Size over all. Height, 44 in., 13½ x 13 in. Weight, 33½ lbs. Price, $6.00.

WILLIAM LEAVENS & CO., Manufacturers, Boston, Mass.

Leavens magazine stands, $150, $250, $250.

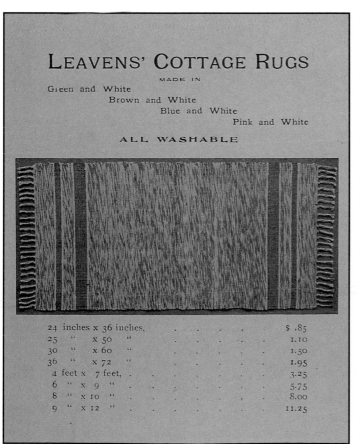

LEAVENS' COTTAGE RUGS
MADE IN
Green and White
Brown and White
Blue and White
Pink and White

ALL WASHABLE

24 inches x 36 inches,	. . . .	$ .85
25 " x 50 "	. . . .	1.10
30 " x 60 "	. . . .	1.50
36 " x 72 "	. . . .	1.95
4 feet x 7 feet,	. . . .	3.25
6 " x 9 "	. . . .	5.75
8 " x 10 "	. . . .	8.00
9 " x 12 "	. . . .	11.25

Leavens cottage rugs, $100 - $500 each.

No. 2015
DUTCH CENTER TABLE, Spanish Leather Top
Solid Oak Legs, any color finish. Price, 36 in., $27.00; 42 in., $31.50; 48 in., $36.00.
No. 2014. Solid Oak Top. 36 in. Price, $21.00. 42 in. Price, $24.00. 48 in. Price, $27.00.

WILLIAM LEAVENS & CO., Manufacturers, Boston, Mass.

Leavens Dutch center table with leather top, $600.

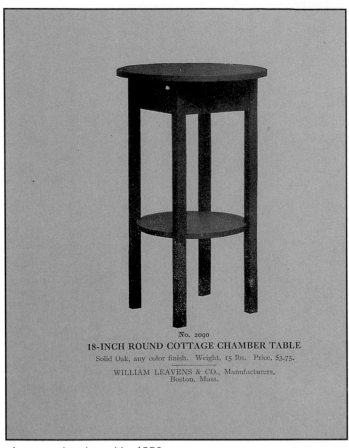

No. 2090
18-INCH ROUND COTTAGE CHAMBER TABLE
Solid Oak, any color finish. Weight, 15 lbs. Price, $3.75.

WILLIAM LEAVENS & CO., Manufacturers,
Boston, Mass.

Leavens chamber table, $250.

No. 2053
UMBRELLA STAND
Solid Oak, Zinc Pan, 15 holes, any color finish. Sizes over all: 20 in. long,
12 in. deep, 29 in. high. Weight, 15 lbs. Price, $6.00.
Also with 10 holes, $6.00.

WILLIAM LEAVENS & CO., Manufacturers,
Boston, Mass.

Leavens umbrella stand, $100.

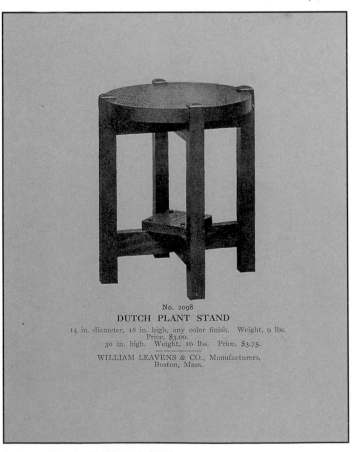

No. 2098
DUTCH PLANT STAND
14 in. diameter, 18 in. high, any color finish. Weight, 9 lbs.
Price, $3.00.
30 in. high. Weight, 10 lbs. Price, $3.75.

WILLIAM LEAVENS & CO., Manufacturers,
Boston, Mass.

Leavens Dutch plant stand, $300.

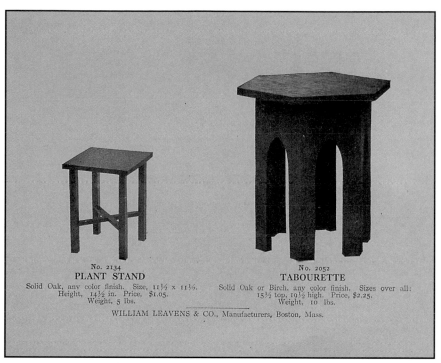

No. 2134
PLANT STAND
Solid Oak, any color finish. Size, 11½ x 11½.
Height, 14½ in. Price, $1.05.
Weight, 5 lbs.

No. 2052
TABOURETTE
Solid Oak or Birch, any color finish. Sizes over all:
15½ top, 19½ high. Price, $2.25.
Weight, 10 lbs.

WILLIAM LEAVENS & CO., Manufacturers, Boston, Mass.

Leavens plant stand, $50, tabourette, $250.

No. 2120
BACHELOR'S CABINET
Solid Oak, any color or finish. Price, $5.25.
Sizes over all: 26 in. long, 17 in. wide, 30 in. high. Weight, 47 lbs.

WILLIAM LEAVENS & CO., Manufacturers,
Boston, Mass.

Leavens bachelor's chest, $650.

SPANISH LEATHER STEERHIDE
and Roan Skins. All colors. Prices on application.
WILLIAM LEAVENS & CO., Manufacturers, Boston, Mass.

Leavens Spanish leather advertising.

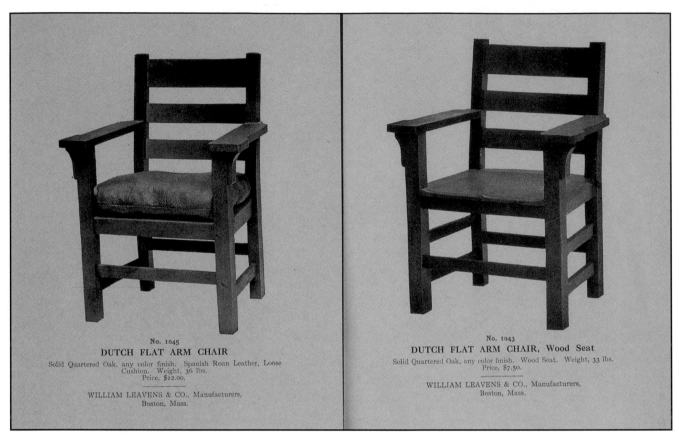

No. 1045
DUTCH FLAT ARM CHAIR
Solid Quartered Oak, any color finish. Spanish Roan Leather, Loose
Cushion. Weight, 36 lbs.
Price, $12.00.

WILLIAM LEAVENS & CO., Manufacturers,
Boston, Mass.

No. 1043
DUTCH FLAT ARM CHAIR, Wood Seat
Solid Quartered Oak, any color finish. Wood Seat. Weight, 33 lbs.
Price, $7.50.

WILLIAM LEAVENS & CO., Manufacturers,
Boston, Mass.

Leavens flat arm chair with leather
seat, $200, with wooden seat, $100.

No. 1083 L. B.
DUTCH ARM
Solid Oak, Spanish Leather Seat and Back, any
color finish. Weight, 30 lbs. Price, $16.50.

No. 1085 L. B.
DUTCH ROCKER
Solid Oak, Spanish Leather Seat and Back, any
color of finish. Weight, 31 lbs. Price, $18.00.

WILLIAM LEAVENS & CO., Manufacturers, Boston, Mass.

Leavens Dutch arm chair and rocker, $250 each.

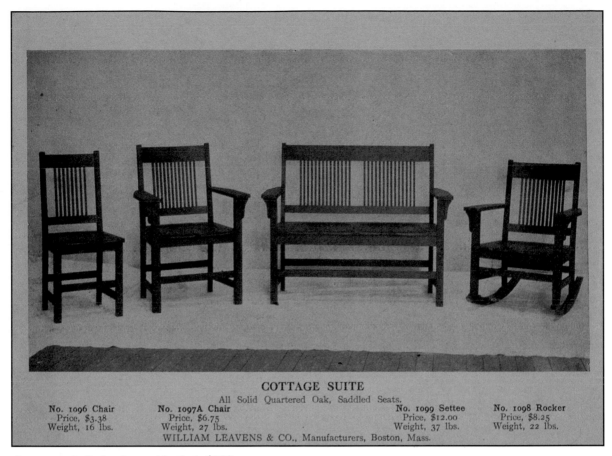

COTTAGE SUITE

All Solid Quartered Oak, Saddled Seats.

No. 1096 Chair	No. 1097A Chair	No. 1099 Settee	No. 1098 Rocker
Price, $3.38	Price, $6.75	Price, $12.00	Price, $8.25
Weight, 16 lbs.	Weight, 27 lbs.	Weight, 37 lbs.	Weight, 22 lbs.

WILLIAM LEAVENS & CO., Manufacturers, Boston, Mass.

Leavens spindle furniture, side chair, $100,
arm chair, $150, settle, $400, rocker $100.

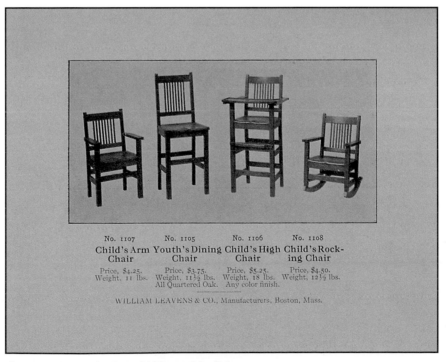

No. 1107	No. 1105	No. 1106	No. 1108
Child's Arm Chair	Youth's Dining Chair	Child's High Chair	Child's Rock-ing Chair
Price, $4.25.	Price, $3.75.	Price, $5.25.	Price, $4.50.
Weight, 11 lbs.	Weight, 11½ lbs.	Weight, 18 lbs.	Weight, 12½ lbs.

All Quartered Oak.   Any color finish.

WILLIAM LEAVENS & CO., Manufacturers, Boston, Mass.

Leavens children's chair, $100, youth's dining
chair, $100, high chair, $150, rocker $100.

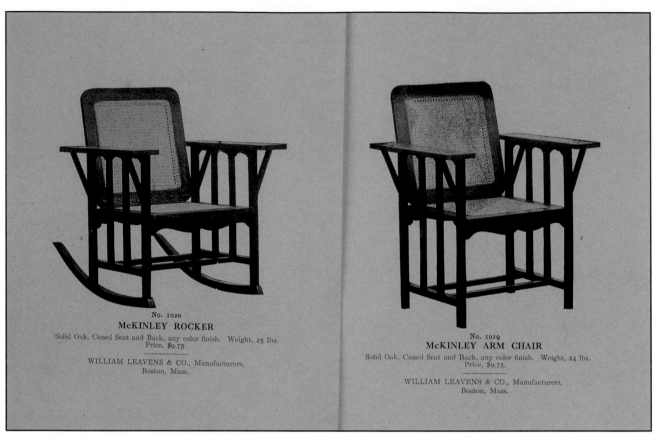

No. 1020
McKINLEY ROCKER
Solid Oak, Caned Seat and Back, any color finish. Weight, 25 lbs.
Price, $9.75.

WILLIAM LEAVENS & CO., Manufacturers,
Boston, Mass.

No. 1019
McKINLEY ARM CHAIR
Solid Oak, Caned Seat and Back, any color finish. Weight, 24 lbs.
Price, $9.75.

WILLIAM LEAVENS & CO., Manufacturers,
Boston, Mass.

Leavens Mckinley rocker and chair, $200 each.

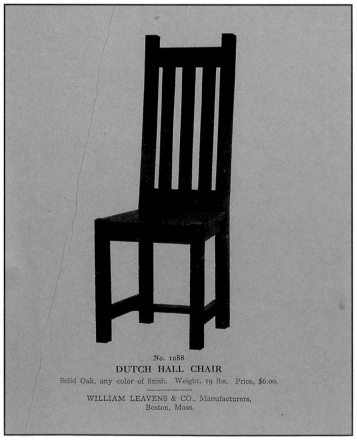

No. 1088
DUTCH HALL CHAIR
Solid Oak, any color of finish. Weight, 19 lbs. Price, $6.00.

WILLIAM LEAVENS & CO., Manufacturers,
Boston, Mass.

Leavens Dutch hall chair, $150.

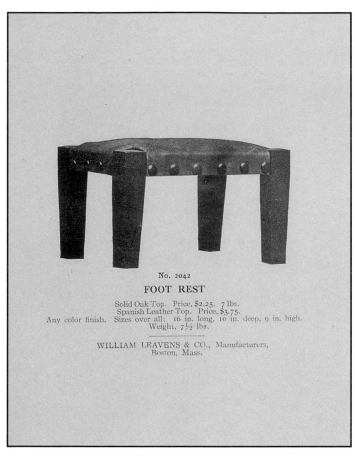

No. 2042

FOOT REST

Solid Oak Top. Price, $2.25. 7 lbs.
Spanish Leather Top. Price, $3.75.
Any color finish. Sizes over all: 16 in. long, 10 in. deep, 9 in. high.
Weight, 7½ lbs.

WILLIAM LEAVENS & CO., Manufacturers,
Boston, Mass.

Leavens foot stool, $100.

No. 2099

DUTCH HALL SETTLE

Solid Oak, any color or finish. Size, 42 in. long, 48 in. high. Width of
seat, 40 in. Depth of seat, 20 in. Weight, 120 lbs.
Price, $18.00.

WILLIAM LEAVENS & CO., Manufacturers,
Boston, Mass.

Leavens Dutch hall settle, $1200.

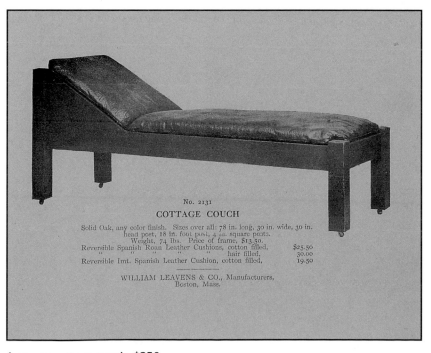

No. 2131

COTTAGE COUCH

Solid Oak, any color finish. Sizes over all: 78 in. long, 30 in. wide, 30 in.
head post, 18 in. foot post, 4 in. square posts.
Weight, 74 lbs. Price of frame, $13.50.
Reversible Spanish Roan Leather Cushions, cotton filled, $25.50
    "   "   "   "   hair filled,   30.00
Reversible Imt. Spanish Leather Cushion, cotton filled,   19.50

WILLIAM LEAVENS & CO., Manufacturers,
Boston, Mass.

Leavens cottage couch, $250.

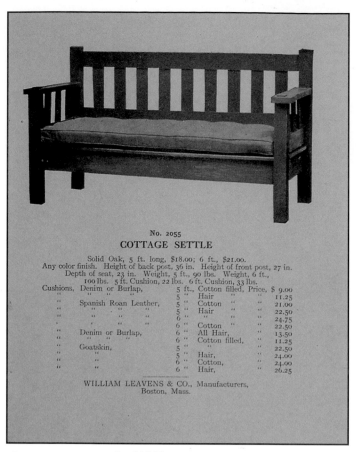

No. 2055
COTTAGE SETTLE

Solid Oak, 5 ft. long, $18.00; 6 ft., $21.00.
Any color finish. Height of back post, 36 in. Height of front post, 27 in.
Depth of seat, 23 in. Weight, 5 ft., 90 lbs. Weight, 6 ft.,
100 lbs. 5 ft. Cushion, 22 lbs. 6 ft. Cushion, 33 lbs.

Cushions,	Denim or Burlap,			5 ft.,	Cotton filled,	Price,	$ 9.00
"	"	"	"	5 "	Hair,	"	11.25
"	Spanish Roan Leather,			5 "	Cotton	"	21.00
"	"	"	"	5 "	Hair	"	22.50
"	"	"	"	6 "	"	"	24.75
"	"	"	"	6 "	Cotton	"	22.50
"	Denim or Burlap,			6 "	All Hair,	"	13.50
"	"	"	"	6 "	Cotton filled,	"	11.25
"	Goatskin,			5 "		"	22.50
"	"	"		5 "	Hair,	"	24.00
"	"	"		6 "	Cotton,	"	24.00
"	"	"		6 "	Hair,	"	26.25

WILLIAM LEAVENS & CO., Manufacturers,
Boston, Mass.

Leavens cottage settle, $1200.

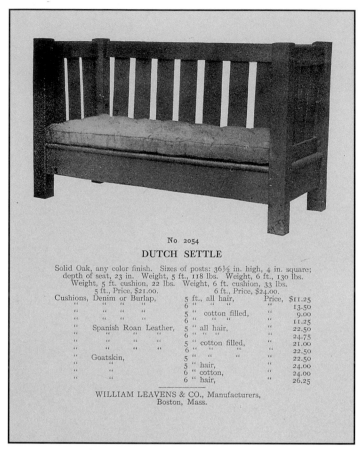

No 2054
DUTCH SETTLE

Solid Oak, any color finish. Sizes of posts: 36½ in. high, 4 in. square;
depth of seat, 23 in. Weight, 5 ft., 118 lbs. Weight, 6 ft., 130 lbs.
Weight, 5 ft. cushion, 22 lbs. Weight, 6 ft. cushion, 33 lbs.
5 ft., Price, $21.00.   6 ft., Price, $24.00.

Cushions,	Denim or Burlap,			5 ft.,	all hair,	Price,	$11.25
"	"	"	"	6 "		"	13.50
"	"	"	"	5 "	cotton filled,	"	9.00
"	"	"	"	6 "	" "	"	11.25
"	Spanish Roan Leather,			5 "	all hair,	"	22.50
"	"	"	"	6 "	" " "	"	24.75
"	"	"	"	5 "	cotton filled,	"	21.00
"	"	"	"	6 "	" "	"	22.50
"	Goatskin,			5 "	" "	"	22.50
"	"	"		5 "	hair,	"	24.00
"	"	"		6 "	cotton,	"	24.00
"	"	"		6 "	hair,	"	26.25

WILLIAM LEAVENS & CO., Manufacturers,
Boston, Mass.

Leavens Dutch settle, $2500.

No. 1047
DUTCH ARM CHAIR
Solid Quartered Oak, Spanish Roan Leather,
Loose Cushion. Any color finish or leather.
Weight, 32 lbs. Price, $12.00.

No. 1048
DUTCH ARM ROCKER
Solid Quartered Oak, any color finish or leather.
Spanish Roan Leather, Loose Cushion.
Weight, 37 lbs. Price, $13.50.

WILLIAM LEAVENS & CO., Manufacturers, Boston, Mass.

Leavens Dutch chair and rocker, $200 each.

No. 1061S
DUTCH ARM CHAIR
With Spanish Steer Hide Seats, any color leather, any oak finish. Made with slip seats, upholstered, or loose cushions.
Weight, 34 lbs.   Price, $15.00.

No. 1062L
DUTCH ARM ROCKER
Weight, 35 lbs.   Price, $16.50.
WILLIAM LEAVENS & CO., Manufacturers, Boston, Mass.

Leavens Dutch chairs and rockers, $200 each.

No. 1061W
DUTCH ARM CHAIR
Solid Quartered Oak, any oak finish. Weight, 33½ lbs.
Price, $8.25.

No. 1062W
DUTCH ARM ROCKER
Solid Quartered Oak, any oak finish. Weight 34 lbs.
Price, $10.50.
WILLIAM LEAVENS & CO., Manufacturers, Boston, Mass.

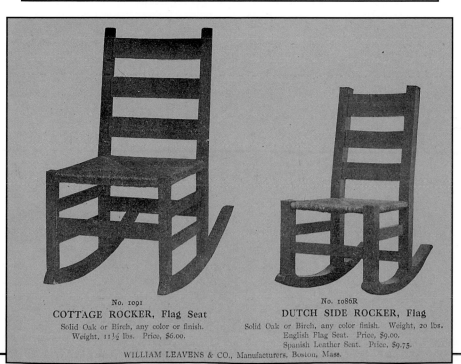

Leavens cottage rockers, $100 each.

No. 1091
COTTAGE ROCKER, Flag Seat
Solid Oak or Birch, any color or finish.
Weight, 11½ lbs.   Price, $6.00.

No. 1086R
DUTCH SIDE ROCKER, Flag
Solid Oak or Birch, any color finish.   Weight, 20 lbs.
English Flag Seat.   Price, $9.00.
Spanish Leather Seat.   Price, $9.75.
WILLIAM LEAVENS & CO., Manufacturers, Boston, Mass.

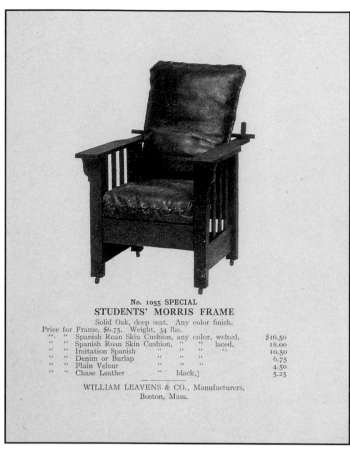

No. 1055 SPECIAL
STUDENTS' MORRIS FRAME
Solid Oak, deep seat. Any color finish.
Price for Frame, $6.75. Weight, 34 lbs.

" "	Spanish Roan Skin Cushion, any color, welted,		$16.50
" "	Spanish Roan Skin Cushion, " " laced,		18.00
" "	Imitation Spanish " " "		10.50
" "	Denim or Burlap " " "		6.75
" "	Plain Velour " " "		4.50
" "	Chase Leather " black,]		5.25

WILLIAM LEAVENS & CO., Manufacturers,
Boston, Mass.

Leavens student Morris chair, $475.

No. 1011
DUTCH MORRIS CHAIR
Solid Oak, any color finish. Weight, frame only, 47 lbs. Cushion,
23 lbs. Price, $13.50.

Cushions, Denim or Burlap, Hair filled,	Price, $ 9.00
Cushions, Denim or Burlap, Cotton filled,	"	6.75
Spanish Roan Leather,	Hair filled,	"	21.00
Spanish Roan Leather,	Cotton filled,	"	16.50

WILLIAM LEAVENS & CO., Manufacturers,
Boston, Mass.

Leavens Dutch Morris chair, $700.

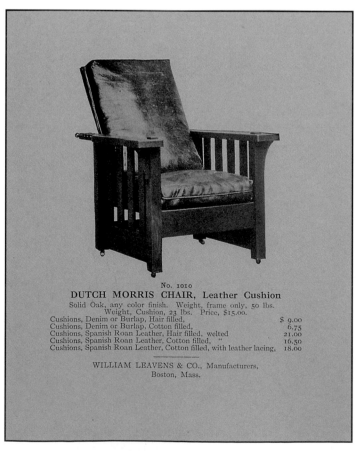

No. 1010
DUTCH MORRIS CHAIR, Leather Cushion
Solid Oak, any color finish. Weight, frame only, 50 lbs.
Weight, Cushion, 23 lbs. Price, $15.00.

Cushions, Denim or Burlap, Hair filled,	$ 9.00
Cushions, Denim or Burlap, Cotton filled,	6.75
Cushions, Spanish Roan Leather, Hair filled, welted	21.00
Cushions, Spanish Roan Leather, Cotton filled, "	16.50
Cushions, Spanish Roan Leather, Cotton filled, with leather lacing,	18.00

WILLIAM LEAVENS & CO., Manufacturers,
Boston, Mass.

Leavens Dutch Morris chair, $1500.

No. 2038
DUTCH DESK, 9 DRAWERS
Solid Oak, any color finish. Weight, 185 lbs. Size, 48 x 30 inches.
Price, $24.00.
This desk has two legs in front not shown in cut.

WILLIAM LEAVENS & CO., Manufacturers,
Boston, Mass.

Leavens Dutch desk, $650.

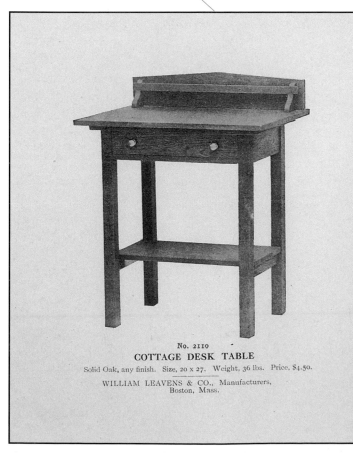

No. 2110
COTTAGE DESK TABLE
Solid Oak, any finish. Size, 20 x 27. Weight, 36 lbs. Price, $4.50.

WILLIAM LEAVENS & CO., Manufacturers,
Boston, Mass.

Leavens cottage desk table, $400.

No. 2194
COTTAGE DESK TABLE
Solid Oak. Any color finish. Price, $22.50. 48 in. long, 27 in. wide,
39 in. high over all. Weight, 138 lbs.

WILLIAM LEAVENS & CO., Manufacturers, Boston, Mass.

Leavens cottage desk table, $750.

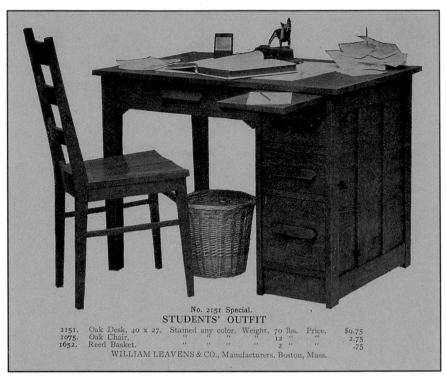

Leavens student desk, $150.

Leavens cottage desk with two drawers,
$300, four drawer desk, $400.

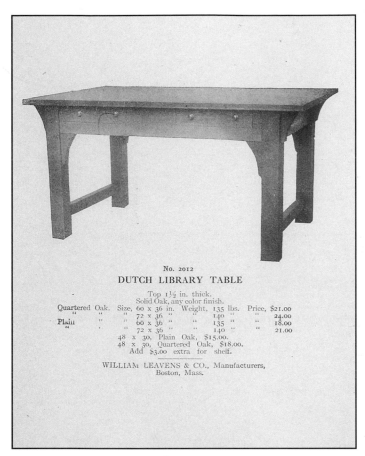

No. 2012
DUTCH LIBRARY TABLE

Top 1½ in. thick.
Solid Oak, any color finish.

Quartered Oak.	Size, 60 x 36 in.	Weight, 135 lbs.	Price, $21.00
"	" 72 x 36 "	" 140 "	" 24.00
Plain "	" 60 x 36 "	" 135 "	" 18.00
"	" 72 x 36 "	" 140 "	" 21.00

48 x 30, Plain Oak, $15.00.
48 x 30, Quartered Oak, $18.00.
Add $3.00 extra for shelf.

WILLIAM LEAVENS & CO., Manufacturers,
Boston, Mass.

Leavens Dutch library table, $300.

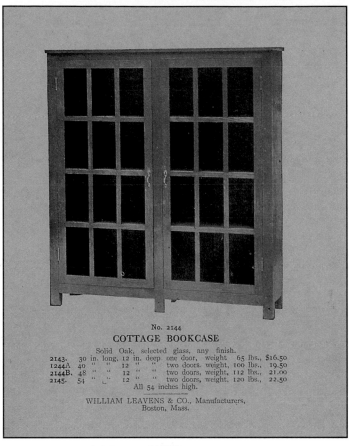

No. 2144
COTTAGE BOOKCASE

Solid Oak, selected glass, any finish.

2143,	30 in. long,	12 in. deep	one door,	weight	65 lbs.,	$16.50
1244A	40 " "	12 " "	two doors,	weight,	100 lbs.,	19.50
2144B,	48 " "	12 " "	two doors,	weight,	112 lbs.,	21.00
2145,	54 " "	12 " "	two doors,	weight,	120 lbs.,	22.50

All 54 inches high.

WILLIAM LEAVENS & CO., Manufacturers,
Boston, Mass.

Leavens cottage bookcase, $1500.

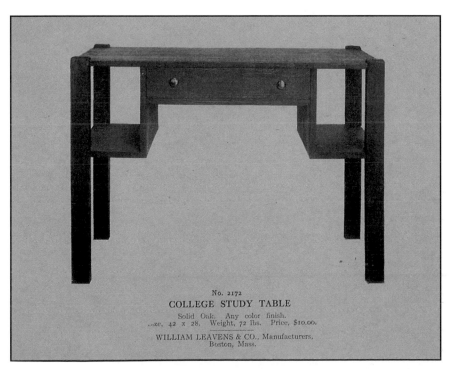

No. 2172
COLLEGE STUDY TABLE

Solid Oak. Any color finish.
Size, 42 x 28. Weight, 72 lbs. Price, $10.00.

WILLIAM LEAVENS & CO., Manufacturers,
Boston, Mass.

Leavens college study table, $150.

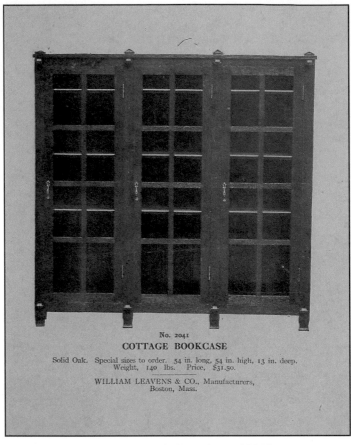

No. 2041
COTTAGE BOOKCASE

Solid Oak. Special sizes to order. 54 in. long, 54 in. high, 13 in. deep.
Weight, 140 lbs. Price, $31.50.

WILLIAM LEAVENS & CO., Manufacturers,
Boston, Mass.

Leavens cottage bookcase with three doors, $2000.

No. 2143
COTTAGE BOOK CASE

Solid Oak, any color finish. Weight, 65 lbs.
30 in. long, 54 in. high, 12 in. deep, $16.50.

WILLIAM LEAVENS & CO., Manufacturers,
Boston, Mass.

Leavens cottage bookcase, $1000.

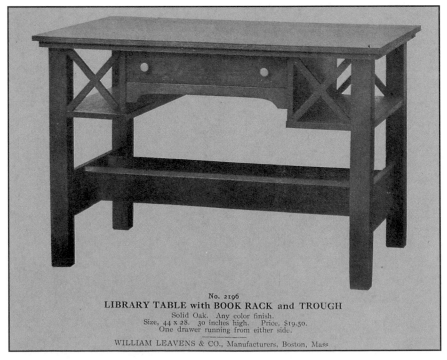

No. 2196
LIBRARY TABLE with BOOK RACK and TROUGH
Solid Oak. Any color finish.
Size, 44 x 28. 30 inches high. Price, $19.50.
One drawer running from either side.

WILLIAM LEAVENS & CO., Manufacturers, Boston, Mass.

Leavens library table, $400.

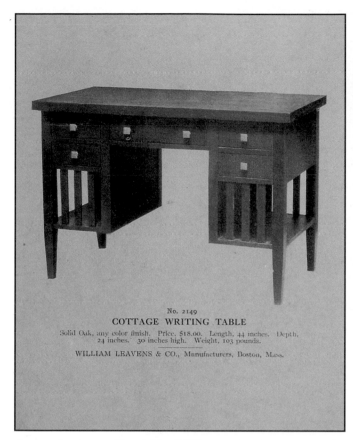

No. 2149
COTTAGE WRITING TABLE

Solid Oak, any color finish. Price, $18.00. Length, 44 inches. Depth, 24 inches. 30 inches high. Weight, 103 pounds.

WILLIAM LEAVENS & CO., Manufacturers, Boston, Mass.

Leavens cottage writing table, $400.

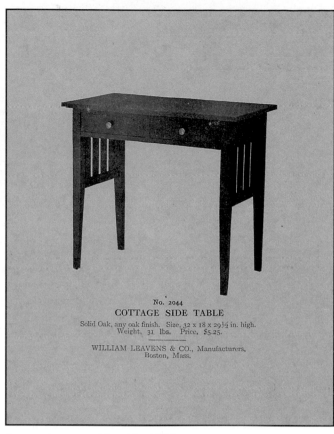

No. 2044
COTTAGE SIDE TABLE

Solid Oak, any oak finish. Size, 32 x 18 x 29½ in. high. Weight, 31 lbs. Price, $5.25.

WILLIAM LEAVENS & CO., Manufacturers, Boston, Mass.

Leavens cottage side table, $300.

No. 2013
DUTCH LIBRARY TABLE, Shelf

Solid Oak, any color finish. Size, 48 x 30 in. Top, 1½ in. thick. Weight, 48 in., 89 lbs. Price, $18.00. Quartered Oak. Other sizes in stock. Plain Oak, $15.00.

WILLIAM LEAVENS & CO., Manufacturers, Boston, Mass.

Leavens Dutch library table, $250.

No. 2023A
COTTAGE LOW BOY, 60 Inches Long
Solid Oak, any color finish. Sizes over all: 60 in. long, 22 in. deep, 44 in. high. Weight, 127 lbs. Price, $30.00.

WILLIAM LEAVENS & CO., Manufacturers,
Boston, Mass.

Leavens cottage low boy, $300.

No. 2022
COTTAGE SIDEBOARD, With Plate Rack.
Solid Oak, any color   Sizes over all: 60 in. long, 44 in. high, 22½ in. deep. Weight, 135 lbs. Price, $35.00.
Brass Knobs used unless otherwise ordered.

WILLIAM LEAVENS & CO., Manufacturers,
Boston, Mass.

Leavens cottage sideboard with plate rail, $650.

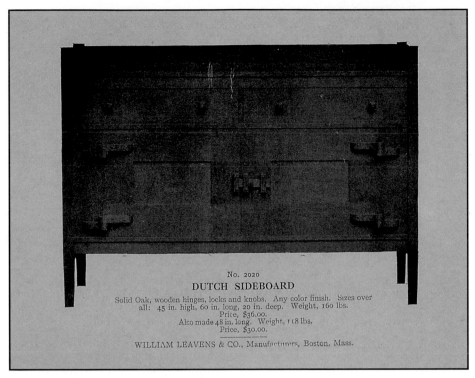

No. 2020
DUTCH SIDEBOARD

Solid Oak, wooden hinges, locks and knobs. Any color finish. Sizes over
all: 45 in. high, 60 in. long, 20 in. deep. Weight, 160 lbs.
Price, $36.00.
Also made 48 in. long. Weight, 118 lbs.
Price, $30.00.

WILLIAM LEAVENS & CO., Manufacturers, Boston, Mass.

Leavens Dutch sideboard, $1500.

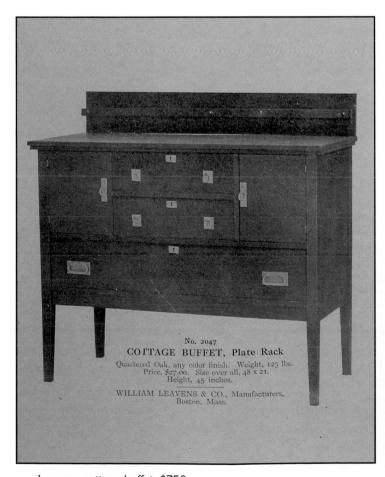

No. 2047
COTTAGE BUFFET, Plate Rack

Quartered Oak, any color finish. Weight, 125 lbs.
Price, $27.00. Size over all, 48 x 21.
Height, 45 inches.

WILLIAM LEAVENS & CO., Manufacturers,
Boston, Mass.

Leavens cottage buffet, $750.

No. 2028
DUTCH SERVING TABLE

Solid Oak, any color of finish.
Sizes over all: 38 in. long, 47 in. high, 18 in. deep.
Weight, 78 lbs. Price, $15.00.

WILLIAM LEAVENS & CO., Manufacturers,
Boston, Mass.

Leavens Dutch serving table, $400.

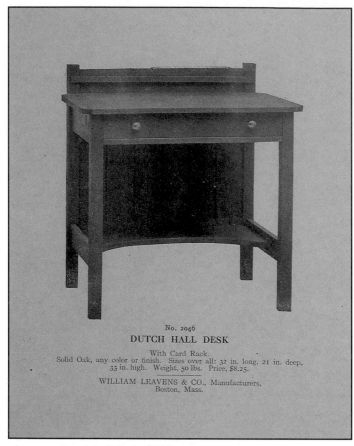

No. 2046
DUTCH HALL DESK

With Card Rack.
Solid Oak, any color or finish. Sizes over all: 32 in. long, 21 in. deep,
33 in. high. Weight, 50 lbs. Price, $8.25.

WILLIAM LEAVENS & CO., Manufacturers,
Boston, Mass.

Leavens Dutch hall desk, $300.

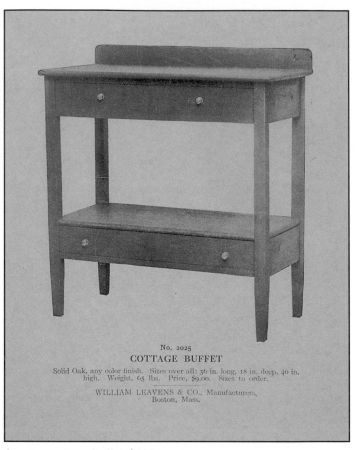

No. 2025
COTTAGE BUFFET

Solid Oak, any color finish. Sizes over all: 36 in. long, 18 in. deep, 40 in.
high. Weight, 65 lbs. Price, $9.00. Sizes to order.

WILLIAM LEAVENS & CO., Manufacturers,
Boston, Mass.

Leavens cottage buffet, $400.

No. 2021
COTTAGE SIDEBOARD

Solid Oak. Sizes over all: 61 in. high, 21 in. deep, 48 in. long, any color
finish. Weight 140 lbs. Price, $32.00.

WILLIAM LEAVENS & CO., Manufacturers,
Boston, Mass.

Leavens cottage sideboard, $500.

No. 1082W
DUTCH SIDE CHAIR
Solid Quartered Oak, Saddled Seat. Any
color finish. Weight, 19 lbs. Price, $4.50.

No. 1082R
DUTCH SIDE CHAIR
Solid Quartered Oak, Genuine Flag Seat.
Weight, 18 lbs. Price, $7.50.

WILLIAM LEAVENS & CO., Manufacturers, Boston, Mass.

No. 1083
DUTCH ARM, WOOD
Solid Oak, any color finish. Weight, 31 lbs. Price, $7.50.
Also made Flag Seat and Spanish Leather.

No. 1083R
DUTCH ARM, FLAG
Solid Oak, any color finish. Weight, 28 lbs.
English Flag Seat. Price, $11.00.
No. 1083. Wood Seat. Price, $7.50.
No. 1083L. Spanish Leather Seat. Price, $12.00.

WILLIAM LEAVENS & CO., Manufacturers, Boston, Mass.

Leavens cottage dining chairs, $100 each.

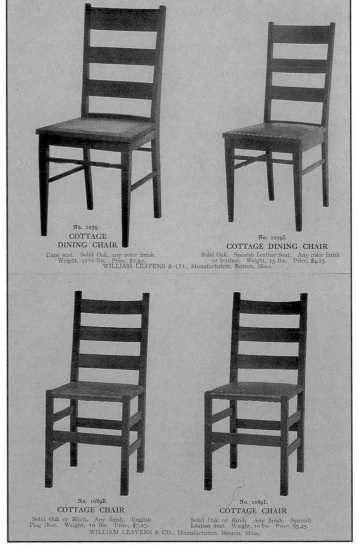

No. 1079
**COTTAGE
DINING CHAIR**
Cane seat. Solid Oak, any color finish.
Weight, 11½ lbs. Price, $2.50.

No. 1079L
COTTAGE DINING CHAIR
Solid Oak. Spanish Leather Seat. Any color finish
or leather. Weight, 13 lbs. Price, $4.25.

WILLIAM LEAVENS & CO., Manufacturers, Boston, Mass.

No. 1089R
COTTAGE CHAIR
Solid Oak or Birch. Any finish. English
Flag Seat. Weight, 10 lbs. Price, $5.25.

No. 1089L
COTTAGE CHAIR
Solid Oak or Birch. Any finish. Spanish
Leather Seat. Weight, 10 lbs. Price, $5.25.

WILLIAM LEAVENS & CO., Manufacturers, Boston, Mass.

Leavens cottage dining chairs, $100 each.

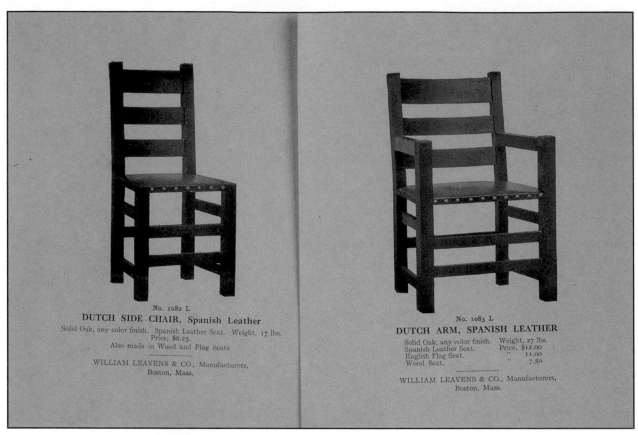

No. 1082 L
DUTCH SIDE CHAIR, Spanish Leather
Solid Oak, any color finish. Spanish Leather Seat. Weight, 17 lbs.
Price, $8.25.
Also made in Wood and Flag Seats.

WILLIAM LEAVENS & CO., Manufacturers,
Boston, Mass.

No. 1083 L
DUTCH ARM, SPANISH LEATHER
Solid Oak, any color finish. Weight, 27 lbs.
Spanish Leather Seat.   Price, $12.00
English Flag Seat.   "   11.00
Wood Seat.   "   7.50

WILLIAM LEAVENS & CO., Manufacturers,
Boston, Mass.

Leavens Dutch dining chairs, $200 each.

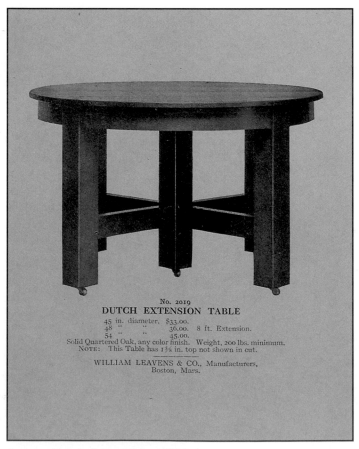

No. 2019
DUTCH EXTENSION TABLE
45 in. diameter, $33.00.
48 "   "   36.00.   8 ft. Extension.
54 "   "   45.00.
Solid Quartered Oak, any color finish. Weight, 200 lbs. minimum.
NOTE: This Table has 1⅝ in. top not shown in cut.

WILLIAM LEAVENS & CO., Manufacturers,
Boston, Mass.

Leavens Dutch dining table, $1500.

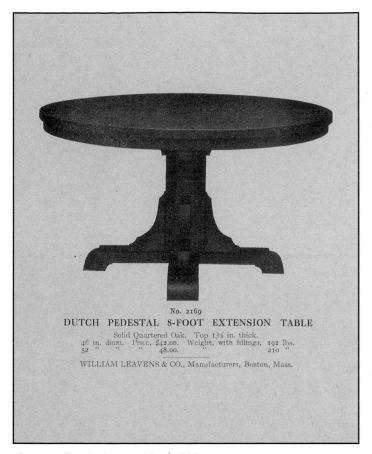

No. 2169
DUTCH PEDESTAL 8-FOOT EXTENSION TABLE
Solid Quartered Oak. Top 1⅜ in. thick.
48 in. diam. Price, $42.00. Weight, with fillings, 192 lbs.
52 "   "   48.00.   210 "
WILLIAM LEAVENS & CO., Manufacturers, Boston, Mass.

Leavens Dutch dining table, $1200.

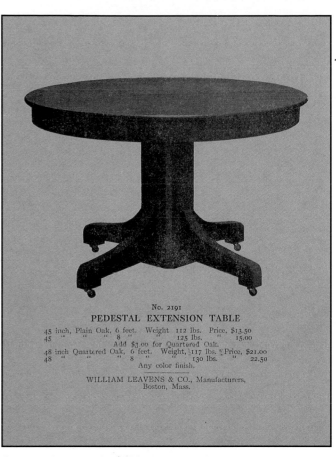

No. 2191
PEDESTAL EXTENSION TABLE
45 inch, Plain Oak, 6 feet. Weight 112 lbs. Price, $13.50
45 "   "   "   8 "   "   125 lbs.   "   15.00
Add $3.00 for Quartered Oak.
48 inch Quartered Oak, 6 feet. Weight, 117 lbs. Price, $21.00
48 "   "   "   8 "   "   130 lbs.   "   22.50
Any color finish.
WILLIAM LEAVENS & CO., Manufacturers,
Boston, Mass.

Leavens dining table, $750.

No. 2166
COTTAGE CHINA CABINET
Solid Oak, any color finish. Price, $30.00.
Size over all: 68 in. high, 38 in. long, 15 in. deep. Weight, 100 lbs.
WILLIAM LEAVENS & CO., Manufacturers, Boston, Mass.

Leavens cottage china cabinet, $1500.

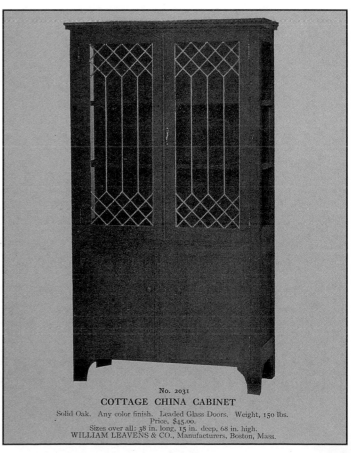

No. 2031
COTTAGE CHINA CABINET
Solid Oak. Any color finish. Leaded Glass Doors. Weight, 150 lbs.
Price, $45.00.
Sizes over all: 38 in. long, 15 in. deep, 68 in. high.
WILLIAM LEAVENS & CO., Manufacturers, Boston, Mass.

Leavens cottage china cabinet, $2000.

No. 2166
COTTAGE CHINA CABINET
Solid Oak, any color finish. Price, $30.00.
Size over all: 68 in. high, 38 in. long, 15 in. deep. Weight, 100 lbs.

WILLIAM LEAVENS & CO., Manufacturers, Boston, Mass.

Leavens cottage china cabinet, $1500.

No. 2192
COTTAGE CHINA CABINET
Solid Oak, any color finish. Price, $15.00. Sizes over all: Height,
59 inches; length, 34½ inches; depth, 15 inches; weight, 95 lbs.

WILLIAM LEAVENS & CO., Manufacturers, Boston, Mass.

Leavens cottage china cabinet, $1200.

No. 2189
COTTAGE BUREAU
Solid Oak, any color finish. Price, $18.00. Sizes over all: 71½ high;
length, 36 inches; depth, 19 inches; height of base, 30½ inches; glass, 36 x
18; weight, 100 lbs.

WILLIAM LEAVENS & CO., Manufacturers, Boston, Mass.

Leavens cottage bureau, $750.

No. 2069
COTTAGE CHIFFONIER WITH MIRROR
Solid Oak, any color finish. Size of mirror, 16 x 20. Sizes over all: 30 in.
long, 18 in. deep, 69 in. high. Weight, 105 lbs. Price, $13.50.
No. 2068. 30 in. long, 18 in. deep, 50½ in. high. Weight, 90 lbs.
Without mirror, $9.00.
WILLIAM LEAVENS & CO., Manufacturers, Boston, Mass.

Leavens cottage chiffonier, $300.

No. 2117
COTTAGE CHIFFONIER, with Hat Box and Mirror
Solid Oak, any color finish. Sizes over all: 30 in. long, 18 in. wide, 70 in.
high; without glass, 51 in. high. Glass, 16 x 20. Price, $14.25.
No. 2118. Without Glass. Price, $9.75. Weight, 98 lbs.

WILLIAM LEAVENS & CO., Manufacturers, Boston, Mass.

Leavens cottage chiffonier, $500.

No. 2138
DRESSER
Solid Oak, any finish. Top, 42 x 16½ in., 36 in. high from floor to top of
dresser; 72 in. high to top of mirror. Size of mirror, plate, 18 x 30.
Weight, 93 lbs.   Price $22.50.

WILLIAM LEAVENS & CO., Manufacturers, Boston, Mass.

Leavens dresser, $500.

No. 2106
COTTAGE DRESSING TABLE
Solid Oak, any color finish. Weight, 112 lbs. Sizes over all:
Length, 44 in.; depth, 24 in.; height, 63½ in.
Price, $17.25.

WILLIAM LEAVENS & CO., Manufacturers, Boston, Mass.

Leavens dressing table, $300.

No. 2141
COTTAGE BUREAU, With Mirror
Selected figured Ash, any color of finish. Weight, 75 lbs. Height, over all,
68½ in. Price, $11.25.
Selected Basswood, No. 2142, any color of finish, $10.50.
Base only, ash, $6.50 Size of top, ash, 39 x 19
Base only, basswood, 5.75 Size of top, basswood, 36 x 17½
Size of glass, 18 x 24.

WILLIAM LEAVENS & CO., Manufacturers, Boston, Mass.

Leavens cottage bureau, $300.

No. 2061
COTTAGE BED
Solid Oak, any color finish. All sizes. Height of headboard, 48 in.
Height of footboard, 36 in. Weight, 3 ft., 86 lbs.; 3½ ft., 90 lbs.;
4 ft., 95 lbs.; 4 ft. 6 in., 100 lbs.
Price, $12.00.

WILLIAM LEAVENS & CO., Manufacturers.
Boston, Mass.

Leavens cottage bed, $300.

No. 2100
INSTITUTION BUREAU
Solid Quartered Oak, Dust Proof Bottom. Special construction.
24 x 30 Glass. Sizes over all: 68 in. high, 40 in. long, 20 in. deep.
Weight, 143 lbs. Price, $24.00.

WILLIAM LEAVENS & CO., Manufacturers, Boston, Mass.

Leavens bureau, $400.

No. 2060
COTTAGE BED
Solid Oak, any color finish. All sizes. Height of headboard, 48 in.
Height of footboard, 36 in. Weight, 95 lbs. minimum.
Price $9.00.

WILLIAM LEAVENS & CO., Manufacturers,
Boston, Mass.

Leavens cottage bed, $150.

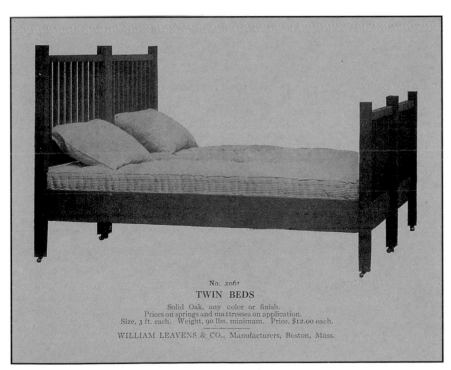

No. 2061
TWIN BEDS
Solid Oak, any color or finish.
Prices on springs and mattresses on application.
Size, 3 ft. each. Weight, 90 lbs. minimum. Price, $12.00 each.

WILLIAM LEAVENS & CO., Manufacturers, Boston, Mass.

Leavens twin beds, $250 each.

No. 2159
COTTAGE BED

Solid Oak, any finish. Price, $13.50. All sizes.
3 ft.   Weight, 100 lbs.   4 ft.   Weight, 112 lbs.
3 ft. 6 in.   Weight, 108 lbs.   4 ft. 6 in.   Weight, 117 lbs.
Height of headboard, 50 in. Height of footboard, 38 in.
Prices on box springs, national springs, pillows, etc., on application.

WILLIAM LEAVENS & CO., Manufacturers, Boston, Mass.

Leavens cottage bed, $300.

No. 2083
STORAGE BUREAU, 5 Drawers

Ash, any color finish. Sizes over all: 34 in. long, 19 in. deep, 56 in. high,
Weight, 92 lbs.   Price, $6.75.
Brass knobs used unless otherwise ordered.
WILLIAM LEAVENS & CO., Manufacturers, Boston, Mass.

Leavens bureau, $500.

No. 2089
COTTAGE WOOD BOX

Solid Oak, any color finish. Weight, 125 lbs. Size of top, with lid down,
26 in. high, 27½ in. deep, 47 in. long. Price, $13.50.
Sizes made to order.

WILLIAM LEAVENS & CO., Manufacturers,
Boston, Mass.

Leavens cottage wood box, $1200.

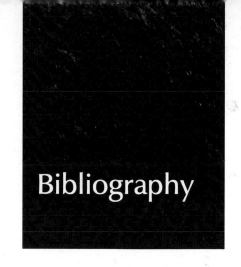

Bibliography

Anderson, Timothy. *California Design 1910.* California: Peregrine Smith, 1980.

Anscombe, Isabelle. & Gere, Charlotte. *Arts and Crafts In Britain and America.* New York: Rizzoli International Publications, 1978.

Austin, Bruce. *The American Arts and Crafts Movement in Western New York 1900-1920.* Rochester, New York: 1991.

Bartinique, A. Patricia. *Gustav Stickley His Craft.* Parsippany, New Jersey: Craftsman Farms Foundation, 1992.

——. *Kindred Styles: The Arts and Crafts Furniture of Charles P. Limbert.* New York, New York: Gallery 532 Soho, 1995.

Boris, Eileen, *Art and Labor: Ruskin, Morris and the Craftsman Ideal in America.* Philadelphia: Temple University Press, 1986.

Bowman, Leslie Greene. *American Arts & Crafts: Virtue In Design.* Los Angeles: Museum of Art, Bulfinch Press/ Little, Brown and Company, 1990.

Brooks, H. Allen. *Frank Lloyd Wright and the Prairie School.* New York: George Braziller, 1984

Cathers, David M. *Furniture of the American Arts and Crafts Movement.* Philmont, New York: Turn of the Century Editions, 1996.

Charles Rennie Mackintosh. Glasgow, Scotland: Richard Drew Publishing Ltd., 1987.

Clark, Robert Judson. *The Arts and Crafts Movement in America 1876 to 1916.* Princeton, New Jersey: Princeton University Press, 1972.

Davidoff, Donald A. & Stephen Gray. *Innovation and Derivation: Contribution of L.&J.G. Stickley to the Arts and Crafts Movement.* The Craftsman Farms Foundation.

Fidler, Patricia J. *Art With A Mission: Objects of the Arts and Crafts Movement.* Kansas City: Spencer Museum of Art, 1991.

Freeman, John Crosby. *The Forgotten Rebel: Gustav Stickley and His Craftsman Mission Furniture.* Watkins Glen: Century House, 1966.

From Architecture to Object: Masterworks of the American Arts & Crafts Movement. New York: Dutton Studio Books, Hirschl & Adler Galleries, 1989.

Johnson, Bruce. *Arts and Crafts: The Early Modernist Movement in American Decorative Arts 1894-1923.* New York: House of Collectibles, Ballantine Books, 1992.

Kaplan, Wendy. *"The Art that is Life": The Arts and Crafts Movement in America, 1875-1920.* Boston: Museum of Fine Arts, 1987.

Lambourne, Lionel. *Utopian Craftsmen: The Arts and Crafts Movement from the Cotswolds to Chicago.* London: Astragal Books, 1980.

Macleod, Robert. *Charles Rennie Mackintosh Architect and Artist.* New York: E.P. Dutton Inc., 1983.

Makinson, Randell. *Greene & Greene Furniture and Related Designs.* Utah: Peregrine Smith Books, Utah, 1979.

Mayer, Barbara. *In the Arts & Crafts Style.* San Francisco: Chronicle Books, 1992

Meech, Julia. & Gabriel Weisberg. *Japonisme Comes To America.* New York: The Jane Voorhees Zimmerli Art Museum, Harry N. Abrams, 1990.

Meyer, Marilee Boyd. *Inspiring Reform: Boston's Arts and Crafts Movement.* Massachusetts: Davis Museum and Cultural Center, 1997.

Morris, Barbara. *Liberty Design.* New Jersey: Chartwell Books Inc., 1989.

Page, Marian. *Furniture Designed by Architects.* New York, New York: Whitney Library of Design, 1980.

Smith, Mary Ann. *Gustav Stickley: The Craftsman,* New York: Dover Publications, 1992.

Trapp, Kenneth R. *The Arts and Crafts Movement in California: Living the Good Life.* New York: The Oakland Museum, Abbeyville Press Publishers, 1993.

Via, Marie & Marjorie Searl. *Head, Heart and Hand: Elbert Hubbard and the Roycrofters.* Rochester: University of Rochester Press, 1994.

Volpe, Tod & Beth Cathers. *Treasures of the American Arts and Crafts Movement 1890-1920*. New York: Abrams, 1988.

Watkinson, Raymond. *Pre-Raphaelite Art and Design*. Connecticut: New York Society Ltd., 1970.

Wilson, Henry. *California Bungalows of the Twenties*, New York, Dover Publications Inc., 1993.

Winter, Robert. *The California Bungalow*. California: Hennessey & Ingalls, Inc., 1980.

Reprints

Arts and Crafts Furniture: The Complete Brooks Catalog of 1912. New York: The Athenaeum of Philadelphia and Dover Publications, Inc., 1993.

Davidoff, Donald. & Robert L. Zarrow. *Early L.&J.G. Stickley Furniture: From Onondaga Shops to Handicraft*. New York: Dover Publications Inc., 1992.

Eastlake, Charles Locke. *Hints on Household Taste*. New York: Dover, 1969.

Gray, Stephen. *A Catalog of the Roycrofters, Some Things For Sale at Our Shop*. New York: Turn of the Century Editions, 1988.

Gray, Stephen. *Arts and Crafts Furniture Shop of the Crafters at Cincinnati*. New York: Turn of the Century Editions, 1983.

Gray, Stephen. *The Mission Furniture of L.&. J.G. Stickley*. New York: Turn of the Century Editions, 1989.

Gustav Stickley After 1909. New York: Turn of the Century Editions, 1995.

Lifetime Furniture. New York: Turn of the Century Editions, 1981.

Limberts Holland Dutch and Arts and Crafts Furniture. New York: Turn of the Century Editions, 1981.

Quaint Furniture Arts and Crafts. New York: Turn of the Century Editions, 1981.

Quaint Furniture. New York: Turn of the Century Editions, 1988.

Roycroft Furniture New York: Turn of the Century Editions, 1981.

Stickley, Gustav. Craftsman Bungalows 59 Homes from The Craftsman. New York: Dover Publications, 1988.